achieve
lasting
happiness

A PRACTICAL GUIDE TO
POSITIVE PSYCHOLOGY

BRIDGET GRENVILLE-CLEAVE

This edition published in the UK
in 2018 by Icon Books Ltd,
Omnibus Business Centre,
39–41 North Road,
London N7 9DP
email: info@iconbooks.com
www.iconbooks.com

First published in the UK
in 2012 by Icon Books

Sold in the UK, Europe and Asia
by Faber & Faber Ltd,
Bloomsbury House,
74–77 Great Russell Street,
London WC1B 3DA
or their agents

Distributed in South Africa
by Jonathan Ball,
Office B4, The District,
41 Sir Lowry Road,
Woodstock 7925

Distributed in Australia and
New Zealand
by Allen & Unwin Pty Ltd,
PO Box 8500,
83 Alexander Street,
Crows Nest,
NSW 2065

Distributed in Canada
by Publishers Group Canada,
76 Stafford Street, Unit 300,
Toronto,
Ontario M6J 2S1

Distributed in the USA
by Publishers Group West,
1700 Fourth Street,
Berkeley, CA 94710

ISBN: 978-178578-385-2

Typeset in Avenir by Marie Doherty

Printed and bound in Great Britain by Clays Ltd, Elcograf S.p.A.

About the author

Bridget Grenville-Cleave holds an MSc with distinction in Applied Positive Psychology (MAPP) from the University of East London, UK, where she specialized in the well-being of professionals, managers and teachers. She is a founder member of the *International Positive Psychology Association* (IPPA) and the *Centre for Applied Positive Psychology* (CAPP).

With her background in business and organizational change and development, she founded Workmad Ltd, which specializes in applying positive psychology at work through training, consulting and coaching. Bridget works with a range of organizations in both public and private sectors, delivering positive leadership, resilience and well-being programmes and positive psychology masterclasses which provide a balance of empirical research and practical tools for personal and professional development. She has designed and developed well-being materials for the UAE Ministry of State for Happiness, well-being curricula for Haberdashers' Aske's School as well as the University of East London MAPP Foundations in Positive Psychology course.

She lectures on the International Masters in Applied Positive Psychology at Anglia Ruskin

University specializing in Positive Psychology for Practitioners, as well as being a regular international speaker at positive psychology conferences. Bridget is an accredited Strengthscope™ assessor and has studied Appreciative Inquiry under Professor David Cooperrider and Quality of Life Therapy under Professor Michael Frisch. She is also an accredited trainer of the award-winning Bounce Back! Well-being and Resilience Programme for children and works with schools across the UK.

Bridget's other psychology books include *101 Activities for Happiness Workshops* (2014) with Emeritus Professor Tom Bourner and Dr Asher Rospigliosi from the University of Brighton; *100 Ways to Happiness: Expert Advice to Feed your Mind, Body and Soul* (Modern Books, 2015) with Dr Ilona Boniwell and the first textbook on *Positive Psychology in Sport and Physical Activity* with Dr Abbe Brady from St Mary's University, London (Routledge, 2017). She is also a Fellow of the Chartered Association of Certified Accountants, a member of the Chartered Institute of Personnel and Development, and has an MBA from the Open University Business School.

Acknowledgements

There are many people I'd like to thank for their help, encouragement and support in writing this book, particularly:

Ilona – for strengths-spotting

Molly and Charlie – making a difference to so many people's lives

Neil and Hugo – step into style!

Karen – a constant source of inspiration

Natasha – kindness itself

Adrian, Alex, Andy, Anish, Caroline, Carrie, Connie, Elise, Jenny, Laura, Lou, Rani, Ros, Naima, Sally, Stefan and Tony – for their support, ideas and case studies

Duncan Heath and the team at Icon Books – for great ideas, advice and feedback.

Author's note

It's important to note that there is much frequently-used research employed in positive psychology.

Where I know the source I have been sure to reference it, but my apologies here to the originators of any material if I have overlooked them.

Contents

Introduction

*Happiness is not achieved by the conscious pursuit of
happiness; it is generally the by-product of other activities.*
Aldous Huxley

What is positive psychology? And why now?

Positive psychology is the scientific study of optimal human
functioning and what makes life worth living. In other
words, it is the psychology of the characteristics, conditions
and processes which lead to flourishing. Researching what
goes right for individuals, communities and organizations
is every bit as important to us as understanding what goes
wrong. Although when positive psychology was originally
launched over a decade ago, it distanced itself from other
branches of psychology, there is no doubt that it has its
roots in the work of William James in the late 19th century,
and humanistic psychology in the mid-20th century, as well
as in the work of ancient philosophers such as Aristotle and
Plato. The main difference is that, as a science, it focuses
on discovering the empirical evidence for thriving. But
it's not science for its own sake – it's the applications that
we're interested in. How can we use empirical research to
improve our own well-being?

It's fair to say that some of the research topics which
now fall under the umbrella of positive psychology are
not new; some even pre-date it. Topics such as optimism,

motivation and emotional intelligence had been studied for many years before positive psychology came along. But there are many other areas of optimal functioning which were under-researched, and about which we knew very little, such as gratitude, hope and curiosity. The vast majority of psychology studies carried out over the past 40+ years have focused on the negative sides of life, such as anxiety, depression, low self-esteem and post-traumatic stress disorder. Positive psychology redresses this imbalance by focusing on the human traits and circumstances which lead to thriving. Although some of the research evidence may seem like common sense, there is a great deal which is new, surprising and even counter-intuitive.

Where does positive psychology come from?

Positive psychology originates from the University of Pennsylvania in the USA, where there is now a Positive Psychology Center (see the Resources section at the back of the book for details). The founders are psychology professors Martin Seligman, who is well-known for his pioneering work on learned helplessness and later on learned optimism, and Mihaly Csikszentmihalyi (pronounced *Me-high Chick-sent-me-high-ee*), best known for his work *Flow: The Psychology of Optimal Experience* (see Chapter 5 for more on flow). The positive psychology movement began around 1998, when Seligman chose it as the theme for his inaugural address as President of the American Psychological Association. Since then, thousands of new research articles and books on the subject have been written, several new academic journals published (for example, the *Journal of Positive Psychology*, the *Psychology of Well-being*, the *Journal of Happiness Studies* and the *International Journal of Well-being*), and an international professional association, the International Positive Psychology Association (IPPA), established.

As yet, over a decade after positive psychology appeared as a formal branch of psychology, there is no sign that our interest in the topics of happiness, well-being and flourishing is diminishing. In fact, the growth in the field, whether in university research projects, conferences and academic degree courses, or in books, blogs and workshops for the general public, gives every indication that positive psychology is here to stay. Even in the last few years, successive British governments have been interested in the idea of developing public policy for well-being, and since 2010 the Office for National Statistics has had a 'Measuring National Well-being' programme which was set up to produce accepted and trusted measures of the well-being of the nation, and the first ever UK All-Party Parliamentary Group on Wellbeing Economics has been established to challenge GDP as the government's main indicator of national success and to promote new measures of societal progress.

In Europe, noteworthy positive psychology players include Dr Ilona Boniwell, course director for the new International Masters in Applied Positive Psychology (iMAPP) at Anglia Ruskin University and former course director at the University of East London's MAPP programme, and Professor Alex Linley, founder and director of the Centre for Applied Positive Psychology. As well as publishing many articles and books on the subject, both combine successful careers in academia with consulting work, applying positive psychology in real-life situations.

About this book

This book has several objectives. Firstly, it aims to provide you with an overview of the most important theories and research findings within the field of positive psychology, whether these are long-established or relatively new topics.

Secondly, this book aims to be of practical use to you. Evidence[1] suggests that around 40 per cent of our happiness is determined by intentional activities, that is, the things we do every day. So this book outlines dozens of different activities and exercises which show you how to apply the scientific findings to your own life, whether at work or at home. These suggestions will give you a good idea of the kinds of things you can do (or stop doing) to improve your well-being.

Thirdly, it aims to be accessible. The first two chapters outline the origins of positive psychology, provide an overview of happiness and summarize the main barriers to well-being. The next five chapters cover the main topics of well-being theory and chapters 8–21 focus on the core elements. You don't have to read every chapter in order; in fact each chapter covers one major topic, and each topic stands alone, meaning that you can pick the book up as and when you have 10 minutes to spare, dip in, and still find something useful, inspirational or thought-provoking.

Finally, I hope this book will be motivating, and that as you read each chapter, you will be encouraged to try new things. Don't be put off by the simplicity of some of the suggested activities. The ease with which you can do them makes it more likely that you'll be successful. It may be the case that some of them do not suit you, and that's fine. We are all individuals with our own personal preferences. But do try to tackle each suggestion with an open mind, and do not pre-judge.

Your own personal scientific experiment?

In 2007, when I was completing the Masters in Applied Positive Psychology at the University of East London, one course assignment was to write a personal portfolio about our own well-being, based on our experience of using some of the positive psychology exercises. As you read *A Practical Guide to Positive Psychology*, I would encourage you to do the same.

1. First of all, get hold of a notebook (or open a new file on your PC or smartphone) to use as a well-being journal in which to record the activities you try and how you get on with them.

2. Then consider assessing your current level of well-being using one of the many happiness, well-being or life satisfaction questionnaires available. You can find several on the Positive Psychology Center's website, including the four-question General Happiness Scale, the five-question Satisfaction with Life Scale and the 24-question Authentic Happiness Inventory. You will get a score for the questionnaires immediately and you'll be able to see how your responses compare to other people's.

   Even if you don't want to take a formal well-being assessment, it will be useful to keep a well-being journal to record your observations and experiences, since you will be able to learn a great deal from your personal reflections.

3. Dip into this book and try out some of the activities. Record how you get on, the impact on your well-being and what you gain. Each activity poses questions on which you might like to reflect, in order to squeeze the maximum benefit from each one.

4. When you finish the book consider re-assessing your well-being using the same questionnaire(s) you used for Step 2. Notice the positive differences that the activities and exercises make to your well-being.

You are in control of your own happiness

Despite the fact that we often talk about *pursuing* happiness, as if it's something 'out there' which we can acquire if we look hard enough, the scientific evidence suggests that happiness is less about 'having' and more about 'doing'. As British psychologist Oliver James pointed out in his book *Affluenza*,[2] it's a mistake to attach your sense of worth and well-being to something transient, like your looks, your job, money or fame, because these things may not last forever. Happiness isn't a passive entity which can be obtained. More exactly, long-lasting happiness can be achieved by changing how you spend your time and your outlook on life. You can do this by trying the activities in this book. It has to be said that this will take time, effort and commitment on your part. The latest psychology research[3] suggests that having the motivation and commitment to improve your well-being, as well as making a consistent effort, are essential in achieving your goal of being happier.

It's also worth remembering that lasting happiness feels much more like run-of-the-mill contentment than unadulterated bliss. Don't expect to set up permanent home on Cloud 9 since it's likely that you'll be disappointed: real life contains many downs as well as ups. A more sustainable strategy is to increase your understanding about what it means to be happy, and to discover and enjoy small day-to-day acts and activities which improve your well-being over the longer term.

So, with that guidance firmly under your belt, read on!

1. What is happiness?

One of the criticisms often levelled at positive psychology is that it's all about the 'big H': happiness. I mean, happiness is a frivolous topic isn't it? Certainly not one worthy of serious scientific endeavour. Yet when you start digging deeper, it becomes clear that happiness is not at all straightforward. In fact, it's a pretty complex concept. In this chapter we'll explore some of the components of happiness (or well-being as it's often called), look at how they're measured and why they matter.

Probably the simplest way to get a handle on happiness is to divide it initially into two basic components:

The distinction between these two aspects of happiness dates way back to the ancient Greek philosophers Aristippus (c. 435–356 BCE), who championed hedonism, and Aristotle (384–322 BCE), who advocated eudaimonism.

According to Aristippus, the goal of life is to maximize pleasure and minimize displeasure or pain. In positive psychology **hedonic well-being** is often used to refer to the happiness you get from feeling pleasure in the moment, pure and simple; it's the 'wine, women and song' variety of happiness, the one which usually springs to mind when you're asked what happiness is. It's typically short-lived though; we have to keep topping up our reserves in order to maintain its effects (see more about this in Chapter 2). One of the problems with defining happiness solely in terms of sensory pleasure is that, paradoxically, some human desires, even if they are pleasure–producing in the short term, are not good for you in the long term.

And what about eudaimonic well-being? If happiness can ever have a serious side, this is it. As we suggested above, some people believe that pleasure on its own isn't sufficient to describe the totality of human well-being. According to Aristotle, merely pursuing pleasure is vulgar; he advocated eudaimonism because he believed that true happiness is found *in doing what is worth doing*, not in having a good time. **Eudaimonic well-being** is a broad term used by positive psychologists to refer to the happiness we gain from having meaning and purpose in our lives, fulfilling our potential and feeling that we are part of something bigger than ourselves.

But even eudaimonic well-being is not problem-free. Some psychologists dislike its moral overtones; they argue that it isn't psychology's job to prescribe what is good for people. And paradoxically, eudaimonic well-being may not provide any pleasurable feelings at all! In fact, it may involve considerable personal hardship and effort over the longer term. Yet it is suggested that eudaimonia leads to greater life satisfaction than pure pleasure alone.[4]

In practice, positive psychologists don't agree on the definition of eudaimonic well-being (terms include 'self-actualization', 'personal expressiveness', 'meaning', 'personal growth', 'engagement' and 'flow'). Nor do they agree on how it should be measured, and often the term eudaimonic well-being is used as a catch-all for any type of happiness that isn't hedonic. But even if we're not yet sure how to define eudaimonic well-being, most people would acknowledge that there's more to true happiness than a few pints in the pub on Friday night and a game of golf on Sunday! Psychology research concurs with this: a recent study of over 13,000 people suggests that pursuing engagement or meaning is more strongly related to well-being than pursuing pleasure.[5]

Another area of disagreement for positive psychologists is whether happiness is a subjective or objective phenomenon. Some definitions of eudaimonic well-being suggest that there is an objective standard against which people's lives can be judged. On the other hand, there are psychologists who insist that happiness is a subjective phenomenon. They argue that it can only be measured by asking people to rate their own happiness. This leads us to another definition of happiness often used in positive psychology – **Subjective Well-Being (SWB)** – which is expressed in the following formula:

Satisfaction with Life + Positive Emotion
– Negative Emotion

In simple terms this means that subjective happiness consists of three elements, one cognitive (or evaluative) and two affective:

Satisfaction with life: what I **think** about my life
(does it measure up to my expectations and resemble
my 'ideal' life?)

plus

The presence of positive emotion: how positive I **feel**

less

The presence of negative emotion: how negative I **feel**

Using Subjective Well-Being as the measure suggests that to increase our level of happiness overall we should focus on minimizing our negative mood and maximizing our life satisfaction and positive mood.

Measuring your Subjective Well-Being
First of all, measure your life satisfaction. You can use Diener and colleagues' Satisfaction with Life Scale.

Then measure how you feel. To do this you can use the Positive and Negative Affect Scale (PANAS) which we look at in Chapter 11, or the Scale of Positive and Negative Experience (SPANE). See the Resources section for details of these assessment tools.

How did you fare? Were you surprised by the outcome? If the results weren't as high as you'd like, how might you increase your life satisfaction and your positive mood, or decrease your negative mood? Write some notes in your well-being journal.

A positive psychology model of well-being

In his most recent book, *Flourish*, Martin Seligman, one of the founding fathers of the positive psychology movement, describes his new theory of well-being. His model (PERMA), which consists of five separate elements, draws on aspects of both hedonic and eudaimonic well-being:[6]

Positive emotion

Accomplishment

Engagement

Meaning

Relationships

Positive emotion is exactly what it says – the experience of positive mood and feelings which are uplifting. As we have already mentioned, there are various questionnaires you can use to measure positive (and negative) emotional states. We'll explore positive emotions, their role in your happiness and their benefits in Chapter 3, and the concept of emotional intelligence in Chapter 11.

Engagement (or 'flow' as it's often called) refers to the well-being you get from being totally absorbed in the task in hand, so much so that you lose track of time and feel completely at one with what you're doing. When sports-people talk about 'being in the zone', they're referring to their experience of flow. Flow is usually measured by asking people to reflect back on their day and record flow experiences or by having them carry an electronic beeper which randomly prompts them to think about and record what they're doing at that moment in time. For more about flow, see Chapter 4.

Relationships are included in Seligman's model because research suggests that good, caring and supportive inter-personal connections are essential to your well-being at any age in life.[7] For more about positive relationships, see Chapter 5.

Meaning is important because it provides both a stable foundation and a sense of direction in life. Pursuing meaningful activities has been found to be more strongly related to happiness than pursuing pleasurable ones. There are many different measures of meaning, although it's still a relatively under-researched area. The Sources of Meaning and Meaning in Life Questionnaire (SoMe) measures 26 different sources, including self-transcendence (such as spirituality), self-actualization (such as challenge and knowledge), order (such as tradition and holding on to values), and well-being and caring for others (such as community and love). For more on meaning, see Chapter 6.

Accomplishment is the latest psychological component in Seligman's well-being model. It's another broad category which includes everything from achievement, success and mastery at the highest level possible to progress towards goals and competence. For more information, activities and insights into accomplishment and its relationship to well-being, turn to Chapter 7.

Now let's explore how these five facets of well-being appear in your life at the moment.

The Wheel of Well-Being

1. Thinking about your life in general, which of your day-to-day activities give you pleasure or joy? Which ones are engaging (put you into flow)? Which ones are centred on building supportive relationships (e.g. with family, friends, colleagues, customers or others)? Which activities are meaningful? And which ones give you a sense of accomplishment, and make you feel that you have made a difference?

2. Once you have formed a snapshot of these in your mind, on a scale of 1–10 rate the pleasure, engagement, positive relationships, meaning and accomplishment in your life, where 1 is 'none or very little' and 10 is 'a lot'. Mark your scores on the Wheel of Well-being overleaf.

   There are no right or wrong answers to this exercise. Its purpose is to encourage you to reflect on how many of the five elements of well-being you experience in your everyday life.

3. Do you have enough of those well-being elements that are important to you? Do you have an imbalance which doesn't feel right, such as a focus on simple pleasure but not enough flow? Perhaps you feel short of more meaningful activities. Or maybe your life is packed with activities which contribute very little at all to your overall

well-being. If your scores are not as high as you'd want them to be, what can you do to increase them? If you're satisfied with your scores, what can you do to maintain the balance which is already working well for you? Jot down your thoughts in your well-being journal.

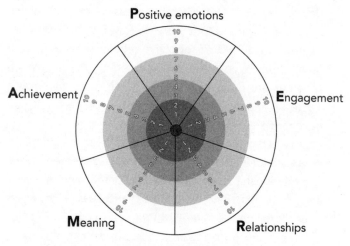

© Copyright 2011, Grenville-Cleave & Akhtar

Wheel of Well-Being (PERMA)

One thing that often comes up when I do this kind of exercise in my training and coaching is that some people feel their lives are lacking in eudaimonic well-being. They experience positive emotions, engagement and enjoy good relationships but when all is said and done, they still feel that something is missing. If this feels like you then there are things you can do about it. Turn to Chapter 6 for more information and activities related to meaning and purpose.

- Happiness is often categorized into two main components, hedonic (sensory pleasure) and eudaimonic (doing what is worth doing, having meaning and purpose).

- Although eudaimonic well-being is not well-defined in positive psychology, there is no doubt that many people feel that there is more to lasting happiness than mere pleasure.

- Subjective Well-Being is used by some psychologists to emphasize their view that happiness is an individual, personal experience, and that psychology should not be prescriptive.

- Seligman's well-being theory has five facets: positive emotions, engagement, relationships, meaning and accomplishment (PERMA).

- How much each of the five facets matters to your well-being is a personal thing.

---

2. Barriers to well-being

In the previous chapter, we looked at various tried and tested pathways to happiness, such as the five components of Martin Seligman's well-being theory: positive emotion, engagement, relationships, meaning and accomplishment. Further details about these pathways to well-being and accompanying activities for you to try can be found in their respective chapters.

But is happiness that easy to attain? Surely if it were simple, we'd all feel pretty upbeat all the time. In practice, there are several psychological obstacles which stand in the way of us achieving long-lasting happiness and content-ment, and it's worth knowing what these are so that we can try to overcome them. In this chapter we'll explore the five main barriers to well-being.

Barrier 1: the negativity bias

The **negativity bias** refers to our tendency to pay more attention and give more weight to negative emotions, experiences and information than to positive ones. In real life this means that you're more likely to remember (and take seriously) an insult, a criticism or a piece of negative information or feedback than a compliment or a piece of positive information or feedback. From an evolutionary perspective this makes perfect sense, since we would not have survived as a species had we not been finely attuned to notice the actual dangers and possible risks all around us. But now that there are far fewer threats in our lives (whatever the media says), this in-built negativity bias can get in the way of our well-being.

Studies also show that positive and negative information of the same importance do not hold equal weight in our minds.[8] If we're given two pieces of equally important information about a stranger, one positive and one negative, they don't balance each other out – we're more likely to form a negative view of the person than a neutral one. Similarly if we have a good experience and a bad experience close together, we'll feel worse than neutral, even if the two experiences are of a similar importance. The evidence suggests that positive and negative emotions are not equal, in other words, negative emotions reduce our level of well-being more than positive emotions increase it. This helps to explain it's important to experience positive emotions frequently. For more information on positive emotions, see Chapter 3.

Psychologist Roy Baumeister and colleagues summed up the impact of the negativity bias in five words: 'bad is stronger than good'.

For the next 48 hours, make a conscious effort to notice and focus on the good things in your life first. As you practise this you will start to shift your awareness from the negative to the positive.

This is one of the principles of the Three Good Things exercise in Chapter 12.

Barrier 2: duration neglect

It seems pretty logical, doesn't it, that the duration of an experience should influence how we feel about it and how we remember it. A two week holiday in the sunshine on a glorious tropical island should feel twice as good as exactly the same holiday in the same location lasting for one week. Likewise, undergoing a negative experience such as a 20 minute dental procedure should feel twice as bad as a 10 minute procedure, assuming we feel the same intensity of discomfort throughout both.

So, it may surprise you to discover that when we evaluate our positive and negative experiences, their duration hardly matters at all, which psychologists call **duration neglect**. Factors which are more important are 1) the *intensity* of the *peak* positive or negative emotion, and 2) how the experience *ends*. So if we undergo a painful medical procedure which lasts 20 minutes, as long as the pain we experience at the *end* is less severe than our worst experience of pain *during* the procedure, we'll actually remember it more favourably than the same procedure in which the worst pain is the same but which is only half as long.

In practice this means that if we want to increase our well-being, and that of other people, we should deliberately look for ways to end experiences on a high note. These can be very simple, as the following examples illustrate:

- If you have a series of unappealing tasks to do, do the least pleasant ones first and leave the most pleasant till last.
- At work, if your team is discouraged by failing to finish a particular task on time, remind them about the tasks that have been achieved so far. Say something like 'At least we've got the hardest part of the job done.'
- If you have to do something like give a presentation at work, make sure you end it on a high, and practise a positive ending until it comes naturally.
- On leaving work at the end of the week, wish colleagues a good weekend.
- Challenge yourself to reframe every bad experience you have this week in a positive way.

During the next week, make a conscious effort to end all experiences on a high note, and notice the difference it makes. Jot down some thoughts in your well-being journal.

Barrier 3: social comparison
We use the expression 'keeping up with the Joneses' to refer to the comparison we make with our friends and neighbours to determine how well we're doing in life. If we buy things to keep up with the Joneses, it means we're not

doing it out of necessity, but as a way of maintaining our social status. So, even if our standard of living is acceptable from an absolute perspective, if it's lower than our peer group our well-being will be diminished.

THINK ABOUT IT

Which of the following two worlds would you prefer to live in?

World A, where you earn $50k a year and others earn $25k a year

World B, where you earn $100k a year and others earn $250k a year

In research, the majority of participants presented with these scenarios chose the first option. In other words, all other things being equal, they'd prefer to be absolutely poorer provided they were relatively better off than everyone else.

Studies such as this one illustrate how important social comparison is to our well-being.[9]

TRY IT NOW!

In the next week, make a deliberate effort to compare yourself with those who are worse off than you, and to appreciate how lucky you are.

If we see people around us (usually family, friends and colleagues) buying more or better stuff than us, it makes us feel worse about our lives. So how much we earn or buy in comparison to others has an impact on our well-being. That others may be up to their eyeballs in debt to acquire all these new goods barely registers. If they've got it, we feel that we've got to have it too. This is all made much worse by celebrity lifestyles which are splashed across the internet, TV and magazines, plus the advertising and brand endorsements which accompany them. The problem occurs because, unbeknownst to many of us caught up in the endless must-have-more cycle, buying more things in an effort to keep up with the Joneses will never make us feel happier. The reason? It's what positive psychologists have dubbed **the hedonic treadmill**.

Barrier 4: the hedonic treadmill
The bad news
Think of the last big purchase you made, the last time you were promoted and got a pay rise, or a brand new company car. Remember how excited and happy it made you feel? Now think how long you stayed excited and happy. A few days? A week? In all likelihood, it wasn't very long. We adapt, we get used to things, whether it's the things we buy or other positive events and experiences in our lives. When that happens, we start taking them for granted, quickly reverting to our usual happiness baseline (also called the 'set-point'). This is what happens when 'the novelty wears off'.

The hedonic treadmill means that, in reality, there's little point in expecting shopping and material goods to raise your well-being permanently. They may give you a little boost of positive emotion in the short term, but the bad news is that it won't last, and you'll soon feel exactly as you did before. Worse still, you may feel driven to buy something else in order to make yourself feel better again. And so it goes on. And on.

Sadly, this adaptation principle also applies to other pleasant experiences or circumstances, such as getting married. In research, the average person does not experience a lasting boost to their satisfaction after marriage. Instead, they experience a short-term increase in happiness, followed by a return to their baseline level beyond the early years.[10]

Potential good news?

On the other hand, this process of psychological adaptation also applies to unfavourable circumstances, which means that if bad things happen, we will feel worse in the short or medium term before eventually coming back up to our baseline or set-point level of happiness. However, research suggests that we adapt much more quickly to positive events and experiences than we do to negative ones.

So there are two take-away messages from the hedonic treadmill story. The first is that you should expect the boost you get from positive experiences like shopping to wear off pretty quickly. The second is that over the longer term it's worthwhile investigating other, more sustainable routes to well-being. And if you're married or contemplating getting married, remember that it's not a guaranteed pathway to permanent happiness – you'll have to work at your relationship continually (for more information and tips on developing positive relationships, see Chapter 5).

Barrier 5: lack of self-control

The fifth barrier to well-being is lack of self-control. Self-control (often called self-regulation) refers to our ability to control our impulses and channel our effort in a way that will allow us to reach particular goals. You're not alone if you think you have low self-control – one study of the 24 character strengths of over 83,000 adults found that self-regulation scored lowest. But self-control is important; according to Mark Muraven and Roy Baumeister, lack of self-regulation is at the heart of many of the social and personal problems that we suffer in the modern, developed world.

Contrary to the popular view that happiness results from giving in to our natural desires, psychology studies show that higher well-being is actually linked to higher self-control. So it makes perfect sense to find ways to increase your self-control. Luckily, self-control is a bit like a muscle, the more you practise it, the stronger it gets. So developing self-control in one life domain can help to strengthen your self-control in other areas.

Find an activity which requires self-control but which you are motivated to do, and practise it regularly.

Examples include:

- keeping a tally of your daily expenditure in a note book or on your smartphone
- improving your posture whenever you become aware of it
- keeping track of what you eat
- practising scales on the piano for 10 minutes every day.

- We naturally give negative emotions, experiences and information more attention than positive ones.

- Negative and positive experiences of roughly the same importance do not cancel each other out – generally the negative experience will affect you more.

- Shakespeare was right – it's true that all's well that ends well! Try to ensure that negative events and experiences end on a high note.

- Comparing yourself upwards is likely to reduce your well-being. Comparing yourself downwards is likely to increase it.

- The novelty almost always wears off!

- Self-control is like a muscle: it improves with practice.

3. Positive emotions

A joyful heart is good medicine.

Proverbs 17:22

Positive psychology's leading researcher in the field of positive emotions is Barbara Fredrickson. She has devoted her academic career to investigating the nature and purpose of positive emotions and testing out her theories under laboratory conditions. We've all come across the 'fight-or-flight' response which accompanies negative emotions. This automatic response mechanism has the effect of narrowing down our thoughts and behaviours to very specific, self-protecting actions; in the case of anger it's to fight, and in the case of fear, to run. But positive emotions are relatively under-researched and not as well understood. There are thousands of academic psychology papers devoted to the experience of fear, for example, and only hundreds on the subject of positive emotions such as compassion.

Fredrickson's goal has been to find out if positive emotions have a purpose apart from making us feel good. Her 'broaden and build' theory suggests that, in contrast to negative emotions which focus us, positive emotions lead to more expansive and creative thoughts and behaviour which create additional personal resources over time.

THINK ABOUT IT

Fredrickson's broaden and build theory suggests that the experience of positive emotions enables individuals to create additional resources in four main categories:

- **Intellectual** e.g. developing our problem-solving skills

- **Physical** e.g. developing our physical strength and cardiovascular health

- **Social** e.g. facilitating the quality and quantity of our friendships and other relationships and connections

- **Psychological** e.g. developing our resilience and optimism.

In short, the experience of positive emotions creates 'upward spirals' of thought and action which prepare you for future challenges.

Other psychologists suggest that experiencing positive emotions also allows you to seek out and work towards new goals.

Fredrickson's research shows that positive emotions don't just feel good, they do us good too.

Three ways to be good to yourself

1. When you're feeling a bit down and in need of a quick pick-me-up, do one of the following for 5 minutes: i) ring a good friend, one who can be relied on to help you look on the bright side, ii) go outside for a walk, preferably somewhere green, or iii) listen to a piece of energising music, anything that will get you tapping your feet or humming along.

2. Create a folder of favourite positive photos on your PC and use them as the screensaver. Every so often when you take a break from your keyboard, a happy image will randomly pop up on the screen and make you smile. Look at the control panel on your PC for instructions. You can also try this on your smartphone.

3. Boost your positive emotions by treating yourself to a special day (out or in), for example a walk in the countryside and a picnic, a visit to an art gallery or a local landmark followed by a nice lunch, a trip to the seaside, a visit to a health spa, a swim, a game of golf or a day devoted to your favourite hobby. Avoid the temptation to spend all day in your PJs, crashed out on the sofa with the remote control, even though this might seem to be the most relaxing way to spend your time. Take

your time planning what you're going to do, take your time to enjoy the day and take your time reminiscing about it afterwards – you can use some of the savouring tips mentioned in Chapter 20. Then try stretching this out into a week of activities – think of something different to do for 15–30 minutes every day which will boost your positive emotions. Ideas include enjoying a luxury bubble bath or dancing round the living room to some of your favourite songs.

Record the activities you do, and how good you felt doing them, in your well-being journal.

Doing good does you good!

Being kind to others by voluntarily performing small acts of kindness is without doubt one of the most important activities for cementing human relationships and building bonds with others, whether they are strangers or family and friends. Positive psychology research provides the empirical evidence that doing kind deeds is good for the doer's well-being, as well as being good for the recipient's.

Perform five random acts of kindness today, for example:

- hold open a door or pick something up for someone
- pay someone a compliment
- give way to another driver

- allow someone to go ahead of you in the supermarket queue
- give up your seat on the tube.

Random acts of kindness also promote 'happiness contagion' – see Chapter 5 for more on how happiness spreads from person to person.

Positive emotions undo negative emotions

Barbara Fredrickson has carried out numerous experiments to recreate positive emotions in people in laboratory conditions and to assess the effect on their minds and bodies.[11] In one study participants were told they had to perform a stressful task. Before completing the task they were divided into four groups and asked to watch a short film clip. These clips provoked emotions such as amusement, contentment, sadness or no feeling at all. The people who felt amused or contented after being told of the stressful task recovered significantly more quickly (as measured by their blood pressure and heart rate returning to normal) than the people who watched the sad or neutral films. As a result psychologists often say that positive emotions have an 'un-doing effect' – they help to counteract feelings of stress and negative emotions. So you can think about positive emotions as an 'inner re-set button'.

Positivity portfolio

Fredrickson recommends creating a range of physical portfolios of objects and mementos to evoke particular positive emotions such as pride, joy and amusement. Collect together items such as photos, gifts, music and letters which make you feel contented, thankful or inspired. You can keep your portfolios on your PC or smartphone, on a webpage, in a scrapbook or in your well-being journal. Look at your portfolios when you need a boost, and enjoy the positive memories they evoke. Keep looking out for new items to include.

The benefits of positive emotions

There are numerous research studies which outline the benefits of longer-term happiness and shorter-term positive emotions. For example, happiness and positive emotions are linked to:

- Living longer
- Higher earnings and getting better appraisals at work
- Sociability and better quality relationships
- Better mental and physical health and ability to manage illness
- Likeability and perceptions of intelligence, competence and physical attractiveness
- Greater persistence and improved performance on difficult tasks
- Creativity

- More efficient decision-making.

The important question for us is whether happiness and positive emotions are the *cause* or the *effect* of these outcomes. The research on this front is less extensive, but nevertheless, there is growing evidence that in many areas, happiness and positive emotions may *lead to* successful outcomes rather than just *following from* them. As a result psychologists conclude that happiness and positive emotions *do* lead to important outcomes such as feeling self-confident, having fulfilling and productive work, satisfying relationships and better mental and physical health and longevity.

Humour diary

Unpublished research by psychologist Willibald Ruch suggests that you can increase your well-being and decrease depression over the longer term by keeping a humour diary. Before you go to sleep write down the three funniest things which happened to you that day. Do this on a regular basis and notice how much your well-being improves. One of the reasons this works is that it draws your attention to funny things (making them more noticeable and less easy to ignore) and away from negative things. You can also give yourself an instant boost of happiness just by dipping into your humour diary and remembering all those funny moments.

Positive emotions good, negative emotions bad?

Of course, we don't want to fall into the trap of thinking that positive emotions are always good and that negative emotions are always bad, as this is simply not the case. For example, getting angry at an injustice can spur you into action. Recent research in positive psychology has started to stress the importance of understanding context.

In the early days positive psychologists got very excited by Fredrickson and Losada's discovery of the so-called '3:1 Positivity Ratio', that is the ratio of positive to negative emotions above which flourishing occurs, and below which we languish. However, recently researchers at the University of East London have demonstrated that the science on which the Positivity Ratio was based is flawed, much to the disappointment of many positive psychologists.[12] All we can say at the moment is that positive emotions are generally more fleeting whereas negative emotions are more 'sticky', experiencing more positive emotions is better (but we cannot put a number on it) and that the *frequency* of positive emotions is more important than their *intensity*.

Let's now think of ways in which we can increase the number of positive emotions we experience. Psychologist Michael Frisch suggests creating a **playlist** of all the activities which interest you and which you've enjoyed in the past. He lists over 200 simple activities including:

- Reading or watching something funny or interesting

- Playing cards or a board game
- Watching the sun rise or set
- Doing something outside
- People-watching
- Flirting
- Writing a poem
- Playing with the kids
- Singing or dancing by yourself
- Staying up late, getting up early, taking a nap
- Putting on comfortable clothes or conversely, dressing up.

In your well-being journal, jot down as many ways as possible that you've played, had fun, relaxed, were creative, forgot your worries, learned something new or contributed to your community. Have some activities which you can do alone, some with a partner and some with a group. Think about inside activities and outside. Go back later and see how many more you can add. You might encourage a friend or partner to do the same, and share your ideas to brainstorm even more.

Now, for 5 minutes every day, engage in some of these favourite activities. Record your most positive experiences, those which really give you a boost, in your well-being journal.

THINGS TO REMEMBER!

- Experiencing frequent positive emotions develops additional personal resources and encourages us to work towards new goals.

- The frequency of positive emotions is more important than their intensity.

- There are a huge number of benefits associated with feeling good and evidence that happiness and positive emotions also lead to positive outcomes.

- Doing little acts of kindness for another person makes you both feel good.

- The 'broaden' aspect of the 'broaden and build' theory of positive emotions suggests that experiencing positive emotions leads to more expansive and creative patterns of thinking and behaving.

- The 'build' aspect of the 'broaden and build theory' suggests that over time, experiencing positive emotions builds upward spirals by developing additional personal resources such as resilience and problem-solving skills.

4. Engagement or flow

Flow is a concept which has been integrated into positive psychology even though it has been around for a great deal longer. Flow, which describes a **state of optimal experience**, was first named and researched by Mihaly Csikszentmihalyi. The two overriding questions on Csikszentmihalyi's mind as he grew up and then emigrated to the USA after World War II were: 'How come some people bounce back from terrible trauma and others don't?', and 'What do you need in order to live a happier life?' He began by studying people who do something for the sheer joy of it, such as dancers, artists and chess players. He discovered that they share very similar 'high-skill high-challenge' experiences, which he called **flow** (sometimes referred to as 'being in the zone', or 'engagement'). Flow is such an important pathway to well-being that it's included (as 'engagement') in Martin Seligman's model of authentic happiness and his well-being theory (see Chapter 1).

In order to experience flow from the activity you're involved in, it has to have the following distinct characteristics:

1. What you're doing is a challenge for you but you feel able to meet it
2. Your goals are clear and you get immediate feedback on how you're doing

3. You feel completely absorbed by what you're doing
4. You feel completely at one with what you're doing
5. You feel in control and you're not concerned about failing
6. You lose track of time (it feels like time passes much more quickly or more slowly than you'd expect)
7. You don't feel self-conscious
8. What you're doing is intrinsically rewarding – you want to do it.

 Find a quiet place to sit for 5 minutes. In your well-being journal make a list of all the activities you've done in the past few days. These might include work, hobbies, socializing, volunteering, housework and so on. Bearing in mind the criteria listed above, which of these activities gives you a flow experience? Think carefully, the answer may not be what you're expecting!

Now set aside some time in the next week to repeat some of your favourite flow activities. Make a note of how you feel afterwards.

The activities which give you flow will be personal to you, but they might include the following:

- Music – playing a musical instrument, listening to music, singing in a choir, conducting

- Creative pursuits – drawing, painting, sculpting, cooking, dress-making

- Sport – playing a team game, climbing, skiing, running

- Other pastimes – dancing, gardening, knitting, gaming, playing chess, building Lego models, reading and so on.

In fact pretty much any daily activity (including work!) can lead to a flow experience as long as it presents a challenge and you have about the right skill level to do it.

The benefits of flow

Experiencing flow is beneficial, not just because it produces positive emotions, but also because it leads to personal growth. Experiencing flow encourages you to persist with challenging tasks and of course this leads to the development of skills. What's more, flow is linked to academic commitment and achievement, better physical health and improved self-esteem.

It should be pointed out that the in-the-moment experience of flow is *not* emotional. In other words, you don't feel any positive emotion *during* the experience itself. Although people typically describe flow as highly enjoyable, this judgment is made after the fact. It is only *after* the experience of flow has ended that you feel invigorated.

A common misconception

Despite its origins and its outcomes, flow *per se* is neither good nor bad. In other words, you can achieve a flow state from doing 'bad' things, like gambling, shop-lifting or reckless driving. What's more, any activity which gets you into flow can become addictive.

Most computer games created these days are designed specifically to induce a flow state in players – that is, they continue to be challenging, yet provide you with instant feedback in the form of points or rewards which tell you how well you're progressing. Once you've mastered one level, you can make it more challenging by going to the next level up.

The ease with which computer games induce a flow state, together with the addictive nature of flow, help to explain why so many gamers want to keep playing and find it difficult to stop.

The important balance between challenge and skill

As I mentioned above, the balance of challenge to skill is essential in creating a flow experience.

High challenge + medium to high skill = flow

If the activity in question is too challenging and your current skill level isn't up to it, you can easily veer off into anxiety and stress. It's quite likely that on your very first day at work you felt something like this – not sure what to do or how to do it. Any new hobby you take up, be it Zumba, playing bridge or watercolour painting, can leave you feeling anxious if the challenge far outweighs your current skill level.

High challenge + low skill = anxiety and stress

So how can you deal with high challenge, low skill situations? Clearly there are two actions you can take – either reduce the level of challenge to something more manageable or increase your level of skill. Can you make the task more achievable by breaking it down into smaller steps? Can you find new ways to increase your skill level, such as taking an introductory course, or reading a beginner's guide? Or perhaps you have hidden talents which you could apply.

 All of us have skills and strengths which we use and rely on every day, but we sometimes forget that they may be transferable from one life-domain to another. You may be a very empathic, patient and caring parent, for example, yet don't think about applying these qualities in the workplace.

Make a list of your best qualities, skills and strengths in your well-being journal, using a table like this one:

Life domain	My best qualities, skills and strengths
Relationships and friendships	
Work	
Home	
Study	
Hobbies	
Other	

Consider how you could apply these qualities when faced with a new high-challenge situation.

Finally, if the activity in question is not demanding enough – in other words, you're already 'over-skilled' for the challenge it presents – you're likely to be overwhelmed by feelings of boredom or apathy.

Low challenge + medium to high skill = apathy and boredom

If this is the situation you're in, try to find ways to make the activity in question *more* challenging and in doing so increase the required skill level. It's relatively easy to make some activities more demanding, for example, you could try to:

- Do them more quickly/against the clock/before the music stops/without a break
- Do them blindfolded!
- Do them in reverse order
- Intentionally avoid all interruptions like email, your mobile phone, snack breaks
- Do them left (or right) handed/with one hand behind your back, and so on
- Do them as a team (if normally done alone, and vice versa)
- Do them quietly (if normally done listening to music, and vice versa).

 Next time you're faced with doing some household chores, set yourself the goal of making them into a flow activity. Typically this will mean finding ways to make the tasks more challenging.

Say today's chore is to wash the car. Estimate how long you would normally spend doing this. Then set yourself the challenge of completing the activity, to the same high standard, with 10 minutes to spare.

Any household chore can be made more demanding. When cooking, you could try estimating every second ingredient, instead of measuring everything. When vacuuming the sitting room, put a favourite CD on and see if you can finish before the end of the track.

How creative can you be?

How to get more flow into your life

There are a number of rules you can follow which will help you get more flow into all domains of your life (not just those pesky chores).

- Set a SMART goal. A SMART goal is one which is:
  - *Specific.* Is your goal well-defined? What exactly do you aim to achieve? 'Swim 40 lengths in an hour twice a week' is a more specific goal than 'get fit'.
  - *Measurable.* You need to make your goal measurable in order to know when it has been achieved.
  - *Achievable.* Make sure the goal is within *your* capabilities.
  - *Realistic.* Is the goal achievable per se? Swimming 40 lengths in an hour twice a week may be doable, but if your job requires you to travel and work away from home regularly then maybe the goal needs to be reworked to take the context into account.
  - *Time-bound.* Have you set a target date and allowed yourself sufficient time to achieve the goal?
- Aim for a high skill/challenge balance (see page 40).

- Focus on what you're doing and minimize likely distractions.
- Find ways to get immediate feedback on your performance.
- Last but not least, make the task fun and enjoy yourself!

 THINGS TO REMEMBER!

- Flow is also known as 'being in the zone' or 'engagement'.

- Flow is one of the five elements of Seligman's well-being theory.

- In order for flow to occur, there are several very specific criteria which need to be in place, such as having clear goals and getting immediate feedback on your performance.

- You can experience flow from a great many everyday activities, including work.

- The key to flow is to find the right balance (for you) between challenge and skill.

- You can find ways to increase or decrease the level of challenge and skill in any activity in order to make flow more likely.

- Often you're not aware of having been in a flow state until after the activity has finished.

---

5. Positive relationships

In today's increasingly materialistic world people frequently make the mistake of believing that they need to own more in order to be happy. You may have heard colleagues in the office on a Monday morning comparing their purchases from the weekend just gone and discussing their shopping trips planned for the next weekend. Add to this the obsession we have with the lives of the rich and famous and it's no wonder that we think we can't be happy until we own that new dress, new car or new house.

Fortunately, research is at hand to help us make sense of well-being and the things which make the greatest contribution to our happiness, as well as explaining why material goods can never make us truly happy (see Chapter 2).[13] One feature which marks out very happy people (i.e. the top 10 per cent) from everyone else is not their money, success or possessions but the fact that they have a good social life, they have friends and a current romantic partner.

So, we know that our connections with others do contribute to both our physical health and psychological well-being. It may surprise you to learn that, according to longitudinal research published in the British Medical Journal, moods and behaviours are contagious, a bit like viruses, and people's happiness depends on the happiness of others with whom they are connected. A friend who lives within a mile and who becomes happy increases the probability that you are also happy by 25 per cent. It makes sense then to focus on what you can do to improve the relationships in your life, and spread a little happiness to others.

According to the most recent American Time Use Survey (2009), on a weekday the average American citizen spends around 30 minutes socializing, and on a Saturday or Sunday between 60 and 75 minutes. Compared with the time they spend watching TV (see Chapter 21), this is nothing! How much time on average do you give to social interaction? If you haven't done the time use exercise in this chapter, make sure you have a guess before you work it out.

Relationships are central to our well-being

Of course, it shouldn't really come as any surprise that warm, trusting and supportive relationships are so important for well-being. As long ago as the 1940s, psychologist Abraham Maslow put love and belonging at the top of his hierarchy of human needs. In the 1960s British psychologist John Bowlby became well known for his work on attachment theory, which describes the importance for an infant of developing emotionally secure bonds with his or her primary carer. In the 1980s the UK psychologist Michael Argyle's work suggested that relationships were one of the most influential factors for our well-being. And more recent positive psychology models of human well-being continue to stress the significance of relationships to our happiness. Richard Ryan and Edward Deci's self-determination theory of human motivation and behaviour recognizes that human relatedness (that is the desire to feel connected to others, to love and care for others as well as to be loved and cared for ourselves) is a primary source of psychological well-being. And now, relationships also have a key place in Martin Seligman's well-being theory (see Chapter 1).

Positive communication

Often when you talk to people about what makes or breaks a good relationship they mention the C word: communication. According to Relate, the UK's most well-known couples counselling service, a breakdown in communication is one of the main reasons why couples seek support. What's interesting is that many of us believe that what is most important in a good relationship is our ability to keep talking constructively to one another whilst managing the *negatives* such as jealousy, conflict and criticism. But do couples give much thought to how they communicate with each other when things are going well for them?

One of the most significant contributions to positive psychology research in the past decade concerns exactly this point. Studies suggest that *our ability to respond enthusiastically to good news in a relationship* is more important than how we communicate with each other during the bad times.[14]

THINK ABOUT IT

Researchers Shelley Gable and colleagues have identified four main styles of responding to good news in a relationship:

Passive Constructive (PC) – you respond to your partner's good news in a rather limp, underpowered and unenthusiastic way. Imagine for a moment that your partner tells you that they've been promoted at work. If you were to respond in a PC style, you might use a low-key phrase such as 'Oh, that's nice', or say something equally subdued, like 'good'.

Passive Destructive (PD) – here you'd respond to your partner's good news of promotion by turning the conversation to yourself. You might say something like 'I had a hellish day today, first of all I missed the bus to work and then I lost my purse as I walked up the High Street.'

Active Destructive (AD) – here you'd give a noticeably negative response, actively quashing their good news. So, in reply to 'Guess what? I was promoted today!', you might say something like 'Oh no, I guess that means more responsibility and more stress! Are you sure you're up to it?' or 'That's terrible, we'll be in the higher tax bracket now and lose some of our benefits.'

Active Constructive (AC) – in the AC mode, you give your partner unbridled enthusiastic and energetic support, allowing them to capitalize on the good news. You might say something like 'Hey, congratulations! What brilliant news! You must feel great! Tell me how it happened?'… 'Tell me all over again what happened? What exactly did your boss say to you? What did you say to your boss? How did you celebrate?' and so on.

Notice that to respond with an AC style you do have to give your partner your full attention, so put away other distractions, turn off the TV, radio or mobile, and allow them to tell you their good news without interruption. It may take some practice before you can respond enthusiastically *and* authentically.

The AC mode is the only way to reply to someone's good news which will help them feel even better about it, and in doing this, you're supporting them and enabling your relationship to flourish.

Which of the four response styles do you recognize in yourself and your significant other? If you don't often use the AC style, try it out with family and friends, and even the man in the corner shop, and notice what a difference it makes to your relationship. Make a note in your well-being journal of how your relationships now start to flourish.

Positive Emotions in Relationships

When it comes to creating strong, happy and long-lasting relationships, extensive research from psychologist John Gottman suggests that we need both positive and negative emotions to be healthy, but that the balance between positive and negative interactions is not 1:1 but 5:1. Five time more positive emotion might seem like a lot, but this doesn't mean that every one has to be an intense experience of high energy positivity such as bliss, delight or ecstasy – it may be lower energy positive emotion such as kindness, amusement or interest. In simple terms, Gottman's research suggests that for a relationship to thrive there must be five times more positive things happening than negative things.

 Take any close relationship you have at the moment, and think back over the past 24 or 48 hours.

How many positive moments, such as times when you laughed together, enjoyed each other's company or helped each other out, can you list? Write them down now.

How many negative moments, such as times when you shouted or got angry with each other, can you recall for the same period of time?

What is the ratio of shared happy moments to unhappy moments? Congratulations if the positive ones outweigh the negative ones, that's a great start!

If your relationship positivity ratio is less than 5:1, however, what might you do to either boost the positives (such as acts of kindness – see Chapter 3) or reduce the negatives? Commit to doing some of those things within the next 24 hours.

Knowing me, knowing you

How well do you *really know* your current partner, or a prospective love interest? My friends Lou and Rani have been married for just over eight years and have two children aged seven and four. Like many couples, they lead very busy lives and often find it hard to balance work and home commitments. 'Couple time', when they can just relax and enjoy each other's company, gets squeezed out. 'We're like ships in the night,' complains Lou, 'we're both so busy either at work or looking after the kids and the extended family that we don't have much time for each other, like we did before we got married. Though I've been avoiding the problem, I think we're drifting apart. I feel as if I don't really know Rani anymore.'

John Gottman, a leading expert on marriage and relationships, suggests that couples who want to build and maintain stronger relationships need to put some time and effort *on a continual basis* into simply getting to know each other. This includes knowing each other's favourite foods, friends and football teams, as well as hopes, dreams and ambitions. Imagine taking part in the old quiz game *Mr and Mrs* and getting all the answers right! Keeping in touch with your partner's wants and needs in this way doesn't have to take up a huge amount of your time either, especially if you do it little and often. Even if you've been with your current partner for many years this is still worth doing. In fact, some would say that it's even more important, because people change, friends come and go and football teams get relegated!

 How many of the following questions about your current partner can you answer straight away?

1. What is their favourite/least favourite film?
2. Who are their two closest friends?
3. What is the first thing they would buy if they won the lottery?
4. What was their favourite/least favourite subject at school?
5. Which two people do they most admire and why?
6. What was their first job?
7. What job would they do if money was no object?

When you first meet someone new you usually feel driven to find out everything you can about them. You're quite likely to ask these sorts of questions and be very eager to hear the answers. As the months and years go by, it's easy to forget to keep up-to-date with your partner's changing likes and dislikes, their wants and needs, so 'getting back in touch' will pay off and help prevent you drifting apart. According to Gottman, really *knowing* your partner is essential in building a long-lasting relationship. He recommends that couples keep in touch with each other by making the time and effort to find out this kind of information on a regular basis.

Why not ask your partner to answer the same questions about you, and talk about the answers?

Then have some fun by taking it in turns to add some of your own questions to the list!

- The desire for connection is a fundamental human need.

- Your relationships (with family, friends, loved ones, colleagues and others) are a central source of well-being.

- People in strong, happy relationships experience five times more positive emotion than negative emotion.

- You can increase the positive emotion or reduce the negative emotion in your relationship to achieve the 5:1 positivity ratio.

- Happiness is contagious. Performing acts of kindness for others can boost your positive emotions, and make others feel good too.

- How you respond to your partner's good news is as important as how you support them in the bad times.

- If your natural response style isn't AC (Active Constructive), keep practising!

- Keeping in touch with your partner's likes and dislikes is essential in building a strong relationship, so make time to find out what they are (and keep asking the questions).

---

6. Meaning and purpose

In Chapter 1 we looked at some definitions of happiness and well-being, including hedonic, subjective and eudaimonic well-being. You may recall that though eudaimonic well-being is still a relatively ill-defined term in positive psychology, it's commonly used to refer to meaning and purpose in life. In Martin Seligman's most recent model of happiness, 'meaning' features as one of the five components of well-being, alongside positive emotion, accomplishment, relationships and engagement.

So, why is meaning so important?

Positive psychology research suggests that meaning performs two central functions in our lives.[15]

Firstly it provides the necessary **bedrock foundation** which enables us to be more resilient and to bounce back from adversity.

Secondly it gives us a **sense of direction**, enabling us to set goals and targets to aim for.

Clinical psychologist, Dr Paul Wong, goes further and suggests that meaning is essential to our happiness and ability to live a good life. He uses the acronym **PURE** to explain his approach to meaning.

P – Purpose. Purpose is all about motivation, and encompasses your goals, values and aspirations. A life without purpose, says Wong, is like a ship without a rudder, you need it for stability and steering. Whilst other aspects of well-being such as personal strengths and self-esteem are important, purpose is key. It's essential for you to have a purpose, whatever it might be.

U – Understanding. Understanding is the cognitive component of meaning which incorporates self-awareness and making sense of who you are, what you do and how you fit into the grander scheme of things.

R – Responsibility. This is the behavioural component which encompasses doing the right thing, acting in a way which is consistent with your values and assuming responsibility for your actions. As Wong points out, if we demand freedom, autonomy and the right to choose, then we must accept the corresponding responsibility for the decisions we make and the actions we take.

E – Enjoyment/Evaluation. This refers to i) the affective (emotions-related) aspect of meaning, in the sense of whether we enjoy the life we lead, and ii) an evaluative component of meaning – if we don't enjoy the life we lead, we need to re-evaluate it and make adjustments.

Fast forward

Purpose is a word often used synonymously with meaning. There are several activities you can do to help uncover your purpose in life. One is to imagine fast-forwarding to the end of your life and to answer the following questions:

1. How, and for what, do I want to be remembered?
2. By whom do I want to be remembered?
3. Which of my accomplishments and personal strengths would I want others to talk about?
4. When I look back, am I satisfied with the life I have lived?
5. Am I living my life in such a way now that this will be achieved?

Answering these questions should help you to start identifying whether you are living according to your values, whether you are achieving your goals, and whether your life is as you wish it to be.

If the answer to questions 4 and 5 is 'no', think about what small changes you can make to ensure that you are heading in the right direction now. What can you realistically do? Which things are within your control? What are you currently doing which will move you towards this goal? It may be helpful to read Chapter 15 on motivation and goals too.

Write down your responses in your well-being journal.

Keep your responses safe and look at them again, say in a few months or a year's time. Ask yourself whether you have made progress towards your goal(s). Feel free to revise your goal(s) as you learn more about yourself and what well-being means to you.

Sometimes people think that their life purpose should suddenly become clear in a kind of epiphany, but according to research it's often a slower process, a gradual realization which takes place over time.

 Psychology theory suggests that there are several different pathways which lead to meaning and purpose in life.

Firstly, you can be proactive and put in the effort over time, gradually refining your life purpose until it becomes crystal clear.

Secondly, you may experience something which changes your life forever, such as the birth of a child or a serious illness. The event may compel you to think differently about what you do and where you're heading.

Thirdly, you may uncover your life purpose through a process of observing other people, perhaps learning from and modelling them.

In order to increase your chances of discovering your purpose, it helps if you're curious and ask questions about things!

For many people, thinking about life purpose can be uncomfortable or seem too abstract. For those of us who are not spiritual, and don't believe in a higher order of things, talking about life purpose can seem airy-fairy. For others, it may mean facing up to some awkward or unpleasant home truths about how we have lived our lives so far. This is quite normal; we are human after all. Nevertheless as the research suggests, believing that you are making a difference in some way, and that your life has purpose, is fundamental to your well-being.

If you feel uneasy thinking about life purpose, a more practical way to get a handle on meaning is to take a step back and consider it in terms of the work that you do. Work can mean formal paid employment, voluntary or community work, or parenting and caring for family. Is your work, whatever it might be, meaningful?

Psychologist Amy Wrzesniewski has been researching meaning in work since the mid-1990s. In psychology, meaning in work is usually explored from two opposing viewpoints: that meaning is determined either internally by our individual personality characteristics or externally by the specific characteristics of the job. Here we take a third perspective, which is less about *you* and the *kind* of job you do, and more about the *relationship* you have to work. Three dominant relationships have been identified:

1. Work as a job – work is merely a means to an end. You don't go to work because you want to, more because you have to. Your job provides the financial resources for you to enjoy your life *outside* of work. If you were

financially secure, you would no longer do this line of work.

2. Work as a career – if we think of our work as a career, we enjoy it but we're focused on promotion to a better, higher-level job and the corresponding rewards such as higher pay, social standing, power and self-esteem. Again, we're motivated by extrinsic factors.

3. Work as a calling – work is an end in itself and it's one of the most important parts of life. If we think of our work as a calling, we don't do it for the rewards or the advancement (although these might be important), but for the contribution it makes to the wider world and for the personal fulfilment it brings. If we see work as a calling, we love our work, and we'd be upset if we couldn't do it anymore.

According to Wrzesniewski, our approach to work and whether we see it as a job, a career or a calling affects our satisfaction with life, and may be more important to our well-being than status and how much we earn. You won't be surprised to learn that viewing your work as a calling is associated with higher well-being.

Job, career or calling?

Reflect on your current work (paid or unpaid). Do you see it as a job, a career or a calling? Have you always thought of work in this way?

Think back to previous jobs you have done, and ask the same question. If your viewpoint changed when you moved from one job to another, can you pinpoint why?

Make a note of your reflections in your well-being journal.

How to give your work more meaning

One study of hospital cleaners illustrates how people can view the same job very differently, with some seeing it as meaningless and some as meaningful. One group of cleaners thought cleaning was mundane and boring; they just did the job according to the job description, and minimized their interaction with patients. They didn't enjoy their work and felt it required few skills. In other words they felt that their work was pretty meaningless. The second group of cleaners 'crafted', or framed, their work in a way which made it meaningful. They took on additional tasks and had more frequent interaction with patients. They enjoyed their job and felt it was important for patient well-being and contributed to the smooth running of the hospital.[16]

Re-crafting your work

How meaningful is your work? If you feel that your work could be more meaningful, think about what small changes you could make to introduce more meaning. An office cleaner who also waters plants when other staff are on holiday or on sick-leave, for example, will create a different relationship with those staff, and this will change the frame of reference for their job.

Amy Wrzesniewski and Jane Dutton suggest three different ways to reframe your work:

1. Change the number, scope and/or type of tasks you do

2. Change the number and/or nature of relationships you have (e.g. with colleagues, customers, patients, students, other stakeholders)

3. Change the way you perceive the job (for example, looking at how it contributes to wider organizational success rather than seeing it as a collection of separate tasks).

Even if you feel that your ability to do 1 and 2 are somewhat limited, you can still do 3.

Psychologists Justin Berg and colleagues suggest asking yourself the following questions:

- If you were given the opportunity to create your own job description within your current organization, what would your responsibilities be?

- How would this 'ideal' job be different to your current job?

- Why do you want to make this change?

- What has stopped you from making this change?

- What would enable you to make this change?

Jot down your ideas in your well-being journal. Take one or two ideas to implement and commit to doing them.

- Meaning is important in life because it provides you with both a stable foundation and a sense of direction.

- Meaning is one of the five components of Martin Seligman's well-being theory.

- Meaning is very personal to the individual. The meaning you get from work may be very different to that of colleagues who do the same job.

- There are several pathways to finding meaning. It doesn't always happen in a grand reveal. It helps to be curious about yourself, about other people and about life.

- If thinking about your life purpose feels like a step too far for you, start by focusing on the meaning of your work instead.

- Re-crafting your job is a way of adding more meaning to your work.

---

7. Accomplishment

Accomplishment is the fifth and final component to be added to Martin Seligman's most recent theory of well-being. It's a pretty broad category, covering everything from achievement, competence and success to progress towards goals and mastery at the highest possible level. These concepts have been studied individually in psychology for decades, but collecting them together under the heading 'accomplishment' within positive psychology is new.

As I mentioned in Chapter 1, positive psychologists don't always agree on definitions of happiness and well-being, nor what should be included in well-being theory and what should be left out. Seligman's original model of 'authentic happiness' consisted of three components: positive emotions, engagement and meaning. In the intervening years, scientific research and debate has inspired him to revise this by adding two further components, relationships and accomplishment.

Accomplishment is included as one of the facets of well-being because like the other components, it is something that humans pursue for its own sake. Even though we all know people who are high achievers for extrinsic reasons, such as increased power, status or pay, accomplishment *per se* is intrinsically motivating. Nurturing accomplishment on its own or together with any of the other four facets, says Seligman, will lead to higher well-being.

We will now look at several different exercises to increase your sense of accomplishment.

The Wheel of Well-being revisited

Take a look back at your response to the Wheel of Well-being exercise in Chapter 1.

Which activities have you done recently that contributed to your sense of competence, mastery or achievement? They may be connected to your work (paid or unpaid) or your personal life (e.g. parenting, caring, hobbies).

Do you get a sense of accomplishment from the things you do day-to-day? If so, from which activities in particular?

Which activities can you do more of to increase the feeling of accomplishment in your life?

Record your responses in your well-being journal.

Accomplishment portfolio

In your well-being journal, draw up a three-column table. In the first column, assign a block of rows to every decade of your life: 0–10, 11–20, 21–30 and so on. Taking each decade in turn, in the second column make a list of all the things that you achieved in those 10 years which made you feel proud then, or make you feel proud now as you look back on them. How you define achievement is up to you. Include all your achievements, big and small. Don't forget that achievement isn't confined to traditional measures of success, such as money, status or qualifications. When you think you've exhausted all the possibilities, spend at least another 5 minutes on this. Think about all the jobs you've done, whether paid or unpaid, all the clubs and groups you've belonged to, as well as all the formal and informal learning you've done.

The chances are that there are far more achievements on your list than you first imagined, and many that you'd completely forgotten about. Now identify the natural abilities, interests or strengths you used to be successful (see Chapter 9). Write them down in the third column. Consider whether any patterns emerge.

Finally, ask yourself how you can use your abilities, interests or strengths this week, at work or at home, in a new way. Record your ideas in your well-being journal. Commit to doing it every day for at least a week. Notice the effect on your well-being at the end of the week.

Accomplishment savouring

Pick one prominent accomplishment from the list you made in the previous exercise, plus a different accomplishment that you haven't thought of in a while. For 15 minutes, reflect on them both, savouring the memory of these achievements (see Chapter 20 for more on savouring).

For each achievement recall what happened, when it happened, and what you did to make this success a reality.

What skills and abilities did you use? What setbacks or challenges did you have to overcome? Who else was involved? What exactly makes you proud of this accomplishment? What positive feelings arise now, looking back on it?

You can also do this exercise with a partner, friend or colleague, taking it in turns to share your two chosen accomplishments. As your partner talks, ask them questions to help them savour their chosen accomplishments even more. Look for ways in which, in the future, they might use the abilities, interests and strengths revealed by their accomplishments.

Accomplishment anchor

You can also use your past successes to give you confidence, spur you on to greater achievements and give you a boost of positive emotions when you need a little psychological pick-me-up. This is an idea adapted from positive psychologist Barbara Fredrickson.

Take your accomplishment portfolio from the exercise on page 66. Over the next 20–30 minutes, find something to remind you of each of the most significant accomplishments. Reminders could include photos of the award ceremony, a sporting trophy, a certificate of achievement, a letter of appointment, a school report, a congratulations card or email from a dear friend, a copy of a sponsorship form showing how much you raised and so on.

Keep these mementos together where you can easily see them, save a digital photo of them on your phone, or create a mental snapshot in your head. When you feel like you need a boost, spend a few moments looking at them, reminding yourself of your significant achievements.

How to increase your level of goal achievement

According to Seligman's theory, achievement can be summarized as follows:

$$\textbf{Achievement} = \textbf{skill} \times \textbf{effort}$$

He suggests that the **skill** and **effort** elements have certain characteristics which are needed for higher achievement:

- **Speed of thought**. According to well-being theory, if you have already acquired a lot of relevant skills or knowledge about a particular task, you won't have to waste brain power on the basics. This leaves you more able to think quickly, and with time left over to devote to planning, checking and being creative. These, of course, are the hallmarks of superior performance.

- **Rate of learning**. Clearly the faster you learn, the more information and knowledge you can acquire per hour spent on the task. This will also put you ahead of the game.

Becoming an expert

In terms of effort, research by psychologist K. Anders Ericsson and colleagues suggests that it takes a minimum of 10 years (or roughly 10,000 hours) of deliberate practice in any subject to become an expert. By 'deliberate practice', Ericsson doesn't mean practising those things which you already know how to do, he means putting sustained effort into the things you can't do very well, or even at all. In other words, in order to become an expert, you have to put yourself outside of your traditional comfort zone, which requires substantial self-motivation and self-discipline.

Since very little is currently known about how to increase our speed of thought and rate of learning, the one thing we can all do to improve our rate of accomplishment is to spend more time on deliberate practice.

If you're serious about becoming an expert in a particular field, Ericsson and colleagues recommend two other tips:

1. Find a coach or mentor who can provide the level of challenge and critical feedback necessary to keep improving your skills
2. Spend time observing a 'master' at work, then copy their techniques.

The role of competence

In Chapter 15 we will talk about competence as one of the three basic psychological needs which increase self-motivation, goal achievement, and well-being. When it's accompanied by perseverance, competence (by which we mean feeling confident, effective and masterful in what we do) makes a good recipe for accomplishment at any level, big or small.

There are several strategies you can adopt to increase your competence in a particular field. One way is to get regular constructive feedback about how you are performing. The feedback might be inherent in the activity: you can tell straight away whether or not you're playing the piano or playing a game of squash well, for example. Or you may have to wait for results, or seek feedback from someone else. If you don't get regular positive and constructive feedback about the things you do, how might you acquire it? Can you identify a mentor, for example?

Another way to increase your competence in relation to your goal is to find ways to improve your skill-set. You could do this by gradually making the goal more challenging, so that you have to strive a bit harder every time you do it. People naturally shy away from stepping outside their comfort zone, but remember, this really is the only way to learn new skills. So when you're feeling uncomfortable, just remind yourself that this is a sign that you have the opportunity to learn something new!

A third method is to undertake specific skills training, either through work or in your spare time. Finally, as Ericsson suggests, you could find a role-model to emulate.

So, those are some of the ways to improve your competence, and increase the probability that you will tread the accomplishment pathway to well-being. You might also like to look at Chapter 14, in which we talk about the role of effort and persistence, which are so essential for goal achievement.

- According to well-being theory, accomplishment is the fifth possible pathway to well-being, alongside positive emotion, engagement, relationships and meaning.

- Accomplishment includes things like achievement, success, competence, mastery, and progress towards your goals.

- Accomplishment can be measured both objectively and subjectively.

- As well as leading directly to well-being, accomplishment can increase your sense of well-being indirectly, for example increasing your positive emotion through reminiscence and savouring your successes.

- Skill and effort are the two main contributors to goal achievement, and you can increase both of these.

- Psychology research suggests that regardless of innate talent, considerable effort is required to become an expert, so practise, practise, practise!

---

8. Appreciative inquiry

What exactly does appreciation mean? And what are we doing when we appreciate something? The interesting thing about the verb 'to appreciate' is that it has several meanings which are relevant to our well-being:

Meaning 1: *to be grateful or thankful for*
Meaning 2: *to recognise the value or quality of something*
Meaning 3: *to increase in value*

In Chapter 12 we explore the importance of gratitude, while Chapter 20 focuses on appreciation from a personal perspective. In this chapter we will look at appreciation from a whole system perspective.

Appreciative Inquiry (AI) is a process for implementing and achieving change which was developed in the 1980s by two American academics, David Cooperrider and Suresh Srivastva. Although it predates Martin Seligman's launch of positive psychology by over a decade, it is often drawn under the same umbrella. In short, AI is a strength-based approach to managing change.

Most change methodologies, whether personal or organizational, tend to start from a negative perspective, by which I mean that you identify what the problem is first, analyse it in detail and then find a solution. One unique attribute of the AI process is that it begins with a positive perspective. In other words, you start by looking at what is currently working well, and build on this information to develop a better, more effective and successful future.

The essence of the AI approach is that focusing on what works well generates the enthusiasm, energy and engagement necessary to recreate the positive and deal with the negative far more effectively than the traditional approach of focusing on the negative alone.

AI is based on five separate principles:

- 'Words create worlds', i.e. reality is not an objective fact, it is a subjective experience. This means that we can change how we view the world, and how we feel, by changing the way we describe our experience, and the stories we tell.
- Asking questions starts the process of change.
- Our individual experience is a story which can be reinterpreted and told in different ways.
- We can create positive change effectively by creating positive images of the future.
- An in-depth review of what went well and what is working now is significantly more enlightening than merely analysing what went wrong.

As its name suggests, AI is about appreciating or valuing the best – whether the best of ourselves, our families, and the organizations we work for, or the places we live in and so on. It's also about promoting further exploration and discovery through being curious and asking questions. This requires us to be open to new possibilities, and creative about making the best of them.

How does AI work?

Before we look in more depth at the four-stage process of AI, a word of warning: it's easy to be persuaded that change is a linear process, along the lines of 'do X, get Y'. However, if you've worked in organizational development or change management, you will know that it's never that straightforward, otherwise the vast majority of change programmes wouldn't fail. The beauty of AI is not just that it uses a simple four-stage process but that it approaches change at a systemic level, that is, it works on the relationships and routines that enable the system to work as it currently does.

This is why David Cooperrider insists on having the 'whole system in the room' in order to make change. In practice this could mean a vast number of organizational stakeholders working on the same issue at the same time. Cooperrider himself has facilitated over 750 Nutrimental Foods employees and stakeholders in one room (a warehouse)! New web technologies enable tens of thousands of people to participate – see IBM's 'jam sessions' for example. It may sound chaotic, messy and unrealistic, but once the logistics are sorted out and the rules of engagement clear, the AI approach to change not only sparks innovation, collaboration and engagement, it is quicker, more energetic and more effective than traditional top-down approaches.

The four stages of AI

As a change process, AI has four separate stages which begin once you have identified your 'affirmative topic', sometimes also called the 'positive core'. In other words you don't begin your appreciative inquiry by thinking about the *problem* that you want to solve, but by focusing on the *positive future* that you want to create instead.

Imagine it's the New Year and you have a resolution to diet or give up smoking. Rather than focusing on 'stopping smoking' or 'losing weight' you might think about saving money, becoming fit, healthy and more energetic, or being able to wear that new red dress. Exploring that goal in more detail, you might describe this positive future image of yourself as one in which you have a spring in your step every day, the confidence to make new friends or the energy to run around the park with your young family.

You can also reframe business goals in the same way. Rather than focusing on 'improving your management skills', which implies a lack, you might re-frame the objective in terms of 'becoming an inspirational leader'. The idea behind this positive re-frame is to find something to work towards. See Chapter 15 for more about approach and avoidance goals.

Once you have identified your affirmative topic, you can proceed to stage 1.

Stage 1: discovery – what's best?

The discovery stage of AI involves asking further positively-framed questions about your affirmative topic, and reflecting on the answers that you come up with. If you're working with others, discovery also involves sharing positive stories related to the topic. Through being curious and asking questions, you begin to create a landscape which will enable a more positive future to emerge.

 Imagine you're feeling demotivated at work, fed up with your job or the organization you work for, and in need of some inspiration. You want to re-capture the positive elements of the role that so inspired you to take up this career in the first place, and re-ignite the sense of excitement you had when you first joined the company.

Try asking yourself the following questions and jot down your responses in your well-being journal:

1. Think about your recent experience at work. Recall a specific incident or event that made you feel extremely satisfied or proud. Describe it briefly, including your role in it and how you felt.
2. What initially attracted you to join this profession/work for this company/do this role?
3. Without being humble, what do you most value about yourself?

4. What are the most important qualities and strengths that you bring to your role? You might like to refer to the activity in Chapter 4 (page 41) if you have already completed it.
5. In what ways does your job contribute to the organization's success?
6. Think of someone else in a similar job who you consider to be a role model. What does he or she do that you so respect or admire?

Your responses will start to lay the foundations for creating a vision in which your role is fulfilling, engaging and energizing.

Stage 2: dream – what's next?

This is where you create a positive and compelling vision of the future, which will be based on the descriptions and stories revealed by the discovery stage. It answers the broad question, 'What might be?'

If the discovery phase is about identifying 'the best' of what you want, and what you most value, the dream phase is about projecting this image into the future, envisioning something which will be even better and starting to create the conditions where this future might start to exist.

 Now think forward to a future, maybe six months from now, when your job is both satisfying and motivating, and you have a real energy and excitement about your work.

What is now different? How has your performance changed? What three things have happened to realize these changes?

_____

_____

 Many coaches use the so-called 'miracle question' to help their clients visualize clearly what this positive future looks and feels like, as well as to start to imagine the part they will play in it.

The miracle question is this:

Imagine that in the middle of the night, when you are fast asleep, a miracle happens and the problems you have been having are solved just like that. But since the miracle happened in the middle of the night, nobody tells you that it happened. When you wake up the next morning, how will you notice that the miracle has happened? What will be different?

You might like to reflect on the miracle question for 5 minutes, and jot down your response in your well-being journal.

Stage 3: design – how might we?
In stage 3 of the AI process you concentrate on answering the question, 'How can it be?' Remember that AI differs

significantly from other change methodologies in that it is rooted in positive images of the past rather than its problems and difficulties. This point is significant, since it helps to ensure that the vision you create in stage 2 is grounded, yet both challenging and motivating. Supporters of AI often like to say that you get more of what you focus on.

 Focus on your image of the future job or role that you most want, and ask yourself the following questions:

- What exactly is happening?
- What are you doing differently?
- What parts of your job would you keep? What would you let go? What would you do differently? What new things would you do?
- Who else is involved? What part are they playing in supporting you? What are they saying or doing?
- What does this positive future look and feel like, in detail?

Record your answers in your well-being journal.

Stage 4: destiny – what will we?

This is where you start the practical work of making your vision into reality. In AI theory, focusing on the positive creates its own momentum, and when it's used in an organizational setting, people will spontaneously progress the topics that they're passionate about. In practice, it may require a project manager or 'AI champion' to keep all the developments on track.

The important message for you to take away is that there is *no one right way* to carry out this stage, hence 'destiny'. Organizations which adopt an AI approach to change frequently develop the capacity to improvise – in other words spontaneously developing and improving by always building positively on what went before.

- AI is a way of making changes which is motivational, inspirational and energizing.

- AI is often used within organizations, but can be used by couples to explore relationships, and by individuals to instigate personal change.

- AI is used by public and private organizations the world over, including Wal-Mart, British Airways, Boeing, the US Navy and the United Nations Global Compact.

- AI has been around since the 1980s but it's still widely accepted as a key positive psychology change tool.

For further information about AI, see the Resources section at the end of the book.

---

9. Character strengths

Character strengths are such an important element of positive psychology that for many people and organizations who work in this field, they have become the central focus of their work, to the exclusion of all other positive psychology topics. One reason is that strengths are such a tangible, concrete subject. When you talk about strengths, people easily grasp what you mean. There's none of the confusion or raised eyebrows that you often get when hedonic or eudaimonic well-being are mentioned (see Chapter 1). And what's more, the language associated with strengths is, by and large, pretty down-to earth.

At the time of writing there are several well-known classifications of strengths.

Firstly there's an assessment of personal, or 'character', strengths: the VIA Inventory of Strengths (VIA-IS, or VIA for short) is probably the best known in positive psychology circles. It's made up of 24 character strengths, such as love, curiosity and social intelligence. The basic online VIA assessment is free and includes a short report showing your strengths in top-down order, with an option to pay a small fee for a more detailed report.

The second model is the Strengthscope™ assessment of work-related strengths. This model is also available online, and assesses the 24 strengths which are most critical to your work performance, such as decisiveness, results focus and collaboration.

Lastly there is the R2 strengths assessment (formerly known as 'Realise2') which spans both work-related and personal strengths, and is based on 60 different psychological attributes including 'listener', 'rapport builder' and 'time optimizer'. For links to these strengths models, see the Resources section at the end of the book.

A misconception about strengths

People often confuse strengths with competencies, talents or skills, but in positive psychology they are not the same thing. For this reason, I've omitted the Clifton StrengthsFinder™ which actually measures the talents that act as the foundations for strengths development, rather than the strengths themselves.

For example, the 24 VIA character strengths differ from competencies, talents and skills in that:

1. They are morally valued in their own right
2. They cannot be wasted.

It's worth remembering that the various strengths models used by positive psychologists do not necessarily define strengths in the same way, so take care.

What is a strength?

In models such as Strengthscope™ and R2, strengths are those personal attributes *which energize us, feel like us and enable us to perform at our best*. It's very likely that your strengths are also the things that you are good at.

When is a strength not a strength?

If you have a competence, talent or skill in something, you are by definition good at it. In positive psychology terms, a strength is *most probably* something you are good at because you use it a lot *but not necessarily!* For example, it could be that you have an 'unrealised strength' (using R2 terminology), that is, a strength which lies dormant, waiting to be discovered and developed to its maximum potential.

To illustrate this, here's the story of my colleague Sally. She's an excellent organizer – if you want an event to run smoothly, whether it's a social event at work, a kid's birthday party or a community litter-pick, she's the woman to ask. She knows exactly who to contact, what to do and how to do it, and she gets it done efficiently and professionally. The right people turn up in the right place at the right time, everyone enjoys themselves and says what a wonderful job she's done.

But does Sally *feel* good about organizing? No! *'I know I'm good at organizing stuff and I can do it with my eyes closed'*, she says, *'that's why people always ask me to do it. And it's pretty easy work, but when I think about it, it doesn't really feel like me at all. And I don't feel energized by it, quite the reverse. In fact I'm absolutely drained by the time it's all over.'* In other words, Sally has a competence in organizing, but it is not one of her strengths.

Identifying your strengths

You can identify your strengths because they:

- Energise you
- Feel like 'the real you'
- Lead to peak performance.

Also, you won't have to force yourself to use your strengths, you'll be intrinsically motivated to do so (see Chapter 15).

What kind of things fit the bill for you? When you are at your best, what are you doing? A great tip from Alex Linley is to look back to your childhood days for clues. So take time to reflect on your early life, remembering the things you loved doing, were good at or found easy to do.[17]

In my case, I've always loved researching and writing – I wrote my first book aged nine, voluntarily completed several research-based projects during the school holidays and nowadays rarely go anywhere without a pen and paper in my pocket.

Remember that your strengths may not always be obvious to you. Sometimes we aren't aware of our strengths at all (i.e. we haven't identified them), or we take them for granted. Often we assume that other people can do the things we do as well as we can.

Alex Linley suggests that another clue to identifying your latent or unrealized strengths is to think about the times when you get frustrated with other people's inability to do things as well or as quickly as you. This may be a sign that you have a strength in this area which you haven't fully recognized.

Benefits of playing to your strengths

There is growing empirical evidence to suggest that using your strengths every day is beneficial to your psychological well-being in a number of different ways, such as:

- **Increased resilience.** People who use their strengths more are better able to bounce back from adversity in their lives.
- **Increased vitality.** Using your strengths is associated with higher levels of positive energy.
- **Decreased stress.** Higher use of strengths predicts lower stress over time.
- **Increased confidence and self-esteem**. Using your strengths more is associated with both increased self-efficacy and self-esteem.
- **Increased happiness**. Using your strengths in new ways is associated with increased well-being over the longer term.

Not only does playing to your strengths improve your well-being, research suggests that it also improves your performance at work, makes you more engaged and more likely to achieve your goals. I'm sure you'll agree that these are very compelling reasons to identify your strengths and start using them more, both at home and in the work-place.

Using your strengths in new ways
Complete the online VIA (see the Resources section for the URL). It's free and the 120 question version takes about 10 minutes to do.

When you receive your online strengths report, cast your eye over the list of strengths. Do you identify with the strengths which appear at the top (say the top 3–5)? Do they feel like the 'real you'? Are you surprised by the ones at the bottom?

Now look at your top strengths, and think about how you might use them in new ways. Here are some of psychologist Chris Peterson's suggestions:

- If love of learning is one of your top strengths, learn and use a new word every day or read a non-fiction book.

- If open-mindedness is a top strength, in a conversation, deliberately argue for the opposite of your private opinion.

- If creativity is a top strength, make up a rhyme for your next text or out of office email message.

- If gratitude is a top strength, write and send a thank you letter (see Chapter 12 for more on gratitude).

- If social intelligence is a top strength, befriend the new member of your team or class, and introduce them to others.

Now that you get the idea, think up your own ways to use your top strengths, and commit to doing so every day for the next week.

If you are reading this book with a partner or friend, why not brainstorm together or pool your ideas? Sometimes it's easier to think of great suggestions for other people.

Carry out some of these new activities using your top strengths and make a note in your well-being journal of the benefits you notice.

 Strengths toolkit

Another good way of thinking about your strengths is as a personal toolkit, an invisible collection of resources which you can draw on at any moment to help you tackle challenges and resolve issues.

Think of an issue that you are currently facing at home or at work. Summarize it in one or two sentences in your well-being journal. Now list your top strengths underneath. Taking each one in turn, think how you might use that strength to deal with the problem in front of you.

For example:

Naima failed to get a promotion recently and she feels upset and demotivated. As a fairly reserved individual, it had taken her a while to get enough self-confidence together to put herself forward, so it's understandable that not getting the job is disappointing. It's starting to affect her performance in the office and she's beginning to wonder if she's even in the right career.

Naima's top VIA strengths are: **perseverance**, **bravery** and **leadership**.

- **Bravery.** She could pluck up the courage to ask the promotion panel for specific feedback about why she was turned down. This might help her better understand what she needs to do to ensure that she will be successful next time.
- **Perseverance.** She could look at the skill(s) she still needs to develop and commit to undertaking some training over the next 6 months, after which she can reapply for promotion.
- **Leadership.** By taking a positive and proactive approach to this issue, she'll demonstrate to the rest of her team how to be resilient in the face of obstacles, and how to learn and benefit in the face of adversity.

Now write down your issue and your ideas for action in your well-being journal and commit to doing them.

You'll find that using your strengths in this way gives you the added confidence, motivation and energy to tackle problems which might otherwise drain you.

Finally, think about what single small change you could make using your strengths that would make the biggest difference at home or at work. Record this in your well-being journal and commit to taking action immediately.

A word about weaknesses

Whist empirical research confirms the long-term well-being benefits of identifying and playing to your strengths, there are two important caveats to take into consideration.

Firstly, it's likely that you'll have strengths in some areas and weaknesses in others. If you complete the VIA Inventory you will know which strengths energize you (the ones at the top of your list) and which ones don't. The ones at the bottom of your VIA list are not necessarily weaknesses, rather they are strengths that you probably haven't used very much because they don't energize you. It may be that you can get through life perfectly well without paying much attention to the ones at the bottom of your list. However, this may not always be the case. If, for example, they include leadership and social intelligence and you work as a team leader, then to be fully effective in the workplace you may need to try to develop them in some way. You could do some additional training, work with a coach or mentor who specializes in that field, or work with colleagues who have complementary strengths which you can draw on as and when you need to.

Secondly, you need to bear in mind that it's possible to overdo or overuse a strength, and when this happens, the strength paradoxically becomes a weakness. Strengthscope™ calls this 'strengths in overdrive'. As an example, if you overuse the strength of courage, you may find yourself taking unnecessary risks or challenges that have a high chance of failure, and friends and colleagues may perceive you as reckless, impulsive or foolhardy. So, it's worth remembering to use a little old-fashioned common sense when considering how and when to play to your strengths!

- Using your strengths has been shown in research to lead to higher well-being over the longer term.

- Using your strengths will not feel like a chore. On the contrary, you will feel excited, eager and exhilarated.

- Playing to your strengths at work leads to improved performance.

- Use common-sense when deciding how and when to play to your strengths in order to avoid overdoing them.

- The basic VIA Inventory of Strengths is free to use, and you'll be contributing to essential academic research in completing it.

- For links to these strengths models, see the Resource section at the end of the book.

---

10. Choice

The more alternatives, the more difficult the choice.

Abbé d'Allainval

It goes without saying, doesn't it, that some choice is good and that more choice is even better? The freedom to choose lies at the heart of any democratic, equal and healthy society based on a free market, ranging from choices as important as who to marry, which school to send our kids to and who to vote for, to choices as mundane as what to eat from the canteen menu, what to wear to work and which TV programme to watch this evening. The flipside of having choice is that we also have to take responsibility for the decisions we make – we're grown-ups after all!

Various studies suggest that feeling that we can control our destiny is vital to our psychological well-being, and that limiting personal choice reduces well-being. There is no doubt that over the past 20 or 30 years we have been seduced by the power of choice, to the point that most of us take it for granted, and don't really give it a second thought. Choice means we have freedom. It means we can express who we are as individuals and it's central to our identity. Denying or restricting choice is considered something to be avoided at all costs. Choice is now central in every domain of our lives, from cradle to grave.

But is having greater and greater personal choice really better for us? Some psychologists believe not, and have shown in research that increased choice makes us unable to make decisions and reduces our well-being. Barry Schwartz, acknowledged world expert on the psychology of choice, states that the fact that some choice is good *doesn't necessarily mean that more choice is better*. Schwartz refers to this as 'the tyranny of choice'.[18]

When you're faced with a seemingly difficult choice, have trouble keeping your choices in perspective, or are feeling overwhelmed by the number of choices facing you, differentiate between those which are really worth the time and effort and those which aren't.

Think about the choice you have to make on a scale of 1–10, where 10 means it's as important as life or death, and 1 means it's relatively unimportant in the grand scheme of things.

For example, choosing a career would be at the top end of the scale, while choosing a new pair of shoes would be at the bottom end.

For unimportant purchases, psychologist Chris Peterson recommends visiting no more than two shops, and allocating no more than 15 minutes to purchases which cost less than £10.

Four decades ago, sociologist Alvin Toffler described a psychological reaction to constant change and too much choice as 'future shock'. He theorized that faced with too much choice – which he called 'overchoice' – in too short a period of time, decisions would be harder and take longer to make as we'd have to process much more information. This would lead to slower reactions and decisions, and ultimately to psychological issues such as depression, distress and neurosis.

Recent psychology research backs this up, suggesting that there are a number of problems associated with having too much choice. For example, in order to make a choice you'll have to make some form of comparison between the different alternatives, which means sifting through an increasingly large amount of information about each one.

Recently I had to make an appointment using the NHS 'choose and book' system. Years ago I'd have just gone to my local hospital; now there are pages of statistics from several hospitals within a 30-mile radius to wade through, including infection and mortality rates, car-parking availability and staff satisfaction rates. In situations like this, even if the majority of the available pieces of information are irrelevant to the choice you're making, you still have to decide whether or not to take each one into account. It goes without saying that the volume and complexity of information you have to deal with increases the likelihood of making the 'wrong' choice or making a mistake. In short, having too much choice causes you to worry, and is likely to lead to lower rather than higher well-being.

Findings from various experimental studies challenge the implicit assumption that having more options is better than having fewer. For example, shoppers are more likely to buy gourmet jams or chocolates and students are more likely to complete an optional class essay when they're offered a limited array of six choices rather than an extensive array of 24–30 choices. What's more, the shoppers reported greater subsequent satisfaction with their selections, and the students wrote better essays when their original set of choices was limited.[19]

Psychology researchers conclude from these studies that having too much choice can have significantly demotivating effects. In relatively trivial contexts, not making a decision, such as going home without buying a pot of jam or a box of chocolates, is neither here nor there. More worryingly, choice overload may hinder decision-making in other more serious contexts, such as choosing medical treatment, especially where there are (or are perceived to be) costs associated with making the 'wrong' choice, and where it takes the chooser a significant amount of time and effort to make an informed decision.

Are you a maximizer or a satisficer?

Back in the 1950s, Nobel prize-winning social scientist Herbert Simon introduced the distinction between maximizing and 'satisficing' as decision-making strategies. A maximizer is someone who wants to make the best possible choice, and so they complete an exhaustive study of all the available options before making their decision. A satisficer, on the other hand, is someone who is looking to make a 'good enough' choice, so they keep looking at options only until they find one which meets their minimum requirements.

It's unlikely that you're 100 per cent maximizer or 100 per cent satisficer, although you'll lean more towards one than the other. If you agree with statements such as '*I never settle for second best,*' and '*Whenever I'm faced with a choice, I try to imagine what all the other possibilities are, even ones that aren't present at the moment*' you're more likely to be a maximizer than a satisficer.

There are significant downsides associated with maximizing, including:

- The time and effort it takes to look at all the available options, which is time and effort which might be better spent in other areas of life.
- Regret that we may not make the best choice.
- Higher expectations – when there's more choice, maximizers tend to expect even more. This can lead to disappointment as things are rarely perfect.
- Lower satisfaction – in the back of the maximizer's mind is always the thought of the better/bigger/faster one that got away.

- Self-blame – maximizers combine high expectations with taking personal responsibility for failure. When things go wrong or don't turn out as expected, there is no-one else to blame but themselves. *'I should have spent longer looking at the options'*, they say.

Although studies show that people who maximize tend to get better, higher-paying jobs than satisficers, at the same time they take longer to settle in and they're more stressed, anxious and frustrated! Maximizers are also more prone than satisficers to be affected by social comparisons and have doubts about their ability compared to others.

 If you think you're a maximizer, psychologists recommend a number of different techniques, including:

- Lowering your expectations. *'Don't expect too much and you won't be disappointed'* may be a cliché, but it's good advice if you want to be more satisfied with life.

- Settling for choices which are 'good enough', especially in trivial areas of life. Once you've made a choice, stop looking!

- Sticking to the choices you make, rather than changing your mind if something better comes up. Chris Peterson recommends throwing away receipts so that you cannot return goods to the shop later.

- Seeing advertising for what it is – a means to get you to part with your money rather than a route towards happiness. Stop reading glossy magazines and watching TV commercials.

- Not buying throwaway products (you only have to find something to replace them when they wear out).

- Practising gratitude (see Chapter 12). Write down three good things about the choice you have made. Be thankful for what you already have in your life.

- Some choice is good for us, but too much choice is not.

- Too much choice can overwhelm us, causing anxiety, stress and ultimately indecision.

- If you are a natural maximizer, you can learn to 'satisfice' (i.e. accept a choice as good enough, rather than the best).

- Maximizers make 'better' choices, but in the long run they are less satisfied than satisficers.

---

11. Emotional intelligence

*Anybody can become angry – that's easy. But to be angry
with the right person, to the right degree, at the right time,
for the right purpose and in the right way – that's not easy.*

Aristotle

Anger is one of those emotions which creates lots of head-
lines. Every week there are news stories of people who've
let their emotions get the better of them, resulting in road-
rage, air-rage or the old-fashioned pub brawl. Surveys suggest that the vast majority of drivers claim to have been
the victim of someone's aggressive driving; it's quite likely
to have happened to you. Rather than give you the benefit
of the doubt for a clumsily-executed manoeuvre (nobody's
perfect!), another driver leaps to the conclusion that you're
deliberately queue-jumping, cutting in or in some way
affronting his masculinity (Home Office reports show that
over 90 per cent of road-rage incidents are perpetrated by
men). They then tailgate you with their lights on full beam
for what seems like miles. And that's if you're lucky! Not
long ago, I witnessed a very ugly instance of road-rage, in
which one middle-aged driver, in some way insulted by the
driving technique of another, deliberately blocked the car
in the next lane at the traffic lights, got out and physically
threatened the other driver with a wooden club. Letting off
steam is one thing, but you can see how moments of blind
fury can lead to actual physical violence.

It's been suggested that it's the way we live in the 21st century which creates more stress than some people are able to deal with effectively. In a recent British survey reported by the BBC, nearly one third of respondents said they had a close friend or family member who has trouble controlling their anger, and 12 per cent admitted that they themselves have the same problem.

The quotation from Aristotle which started this chapter helps explain emotional intelligence (or EI) very neatly. It's not that emotionally intelligent people *never* feel angry (or afraid, or nervous or any other negative emotion for that matter); anger is after all, a natural human emotion without which we would not have survived. It's more that emotionally intelligent people have greater awareness of their own and other people's emotions; they notice how they (and others) are feeling and take these emotions into account when choosing what to do. In short, emotionally intelligent people are self-aware, self-managed, socially-aware and socially-skilled. On top of this, emotional intelligence is linked with several other favourable outcomes, including well-being, more positive moods, and self-esteem, as well as higher leadership performance, better relationships and even less smoking and alcohol-use.

The original concept of emotional intelligence, which is widely attributed to American psychologists John D. Mayer and Peter Salovey, dates from the late 1980s, and was popularized by Daniel Goleman in the 90s. Some two decades on, many different models of emotional intelligence exist, most of which are based on four similar skills:

1. **Identifying** emotions (your own and other people's)
2. **Using** emotions appropriately, to help you think in different ways (e.g. to aid creativity or problem-solving)
3. **Understanding** the causes of emotions
4. **Managing** your emotions effectively.

Notice that EI has interpersonal as well as intrapersonal features.

Name that emotion!

How good are you at identifying your own feelings?

Find somewhere quiet to sit where you won't be disturbed for a few minutes. Think about how you are feeling at this very moment in time. Are you calm? Interested? Worried? Nervous? Excited? Can you name your emotion, or emotions, accurately?

If you are not feeling negative, notice that it doesn't necessarily mean you're therefore feeling on top of the world. Notice also that you can feel positive and negative emotions at the same time.

Why not complete either the:

PANAS (Positive and Negative Affect Scale) by registering at the University of Pennsylvania's Positive Psychology Center website. This measures your levels of positive and negative emotions separately, and allows you to see how you score relative to other people of your age, gender, occupation or postcode.

Or the:

SPANE (Scale of Positive and Negative Experiences) which you can find on Ed Diener's website here: internal .psychology.illinois.edu/~ediener/SPANE.html

Being able to pinpoint your own feelings is the first step in becoming more emotionally intelligent. Every day, set aside a few minutes to practise this skill.

Being able to **accurately recognize** your own emotions is one thing, but can you identify other people's? Think of a time recently when you've had a disagreement with a friend or colleague – can you say how that person felt at the time? And how they felt a few days later?

 Next time you settle down to watch an episode of your favourite soap, record it, and watch 10 or 15 minutes with the sound turned off.

What emotions do you recognize just from looking at the characters' faces? Make a note of the character and their emotion.

Then watch the recording you made, this time with the sound turned on. How accurate was your assessment of the characters' emotions?

You can practise spotting others' emotions wherever you see people interacting, for example, friends chatting at the bus stop, colleagues eating lunch in the office canteen, customers returning goods they've bought, a mother and her child playing in the park, and so on.

Make a point of focusing on faces to improve your ability to identify emotions.

Emotionally intelligent people also **know how to use** their emotions (and those of other people). They understand how feelings influence thinking and behaviour, and therefore know how to use emotions effectively.

Positive psychology studies suggest that positive and negative moods influence our thinking in very different ways.

Negative feelings:
• Make us more focused
• Make it easier for us to be critical
• Make us more likely to spot mistakes
• Make it easier for us to pay attention to detail.

Positive feelings:
• Expand our thinking
• Make it easier for us to think up new ideas
• Encourage us to consider new possibilities
• Help us think in terms of opportunities rather than problems.

You may wish to revisit Chapter 3 which talks more about positive emotions.

According to Albert Ellis, the American psychologist widely credited (along with Aaron T. Beck) with devising cognitive behavioural therapy (CBT), certain thoughts and beliefs also lead to specific emotions, which then lead to specific types of behaviour, as shown in the table opposite.

Understanding emotions is also a sign of an emotionally intelligent person. People with high emotional intelligence are aware (often intuitively) of the connections between thoughts, beliefs, feelings and behaviours. They use this information to make sense of why they, and other people, feel the way they do. They understand what causes certain emotions, how emotions are linked together, and how one can lead to another. Put together, this means *they can predict emotional reactions*. In terms of our ability to keep a handle on our own moods, this is an extremely useful skill to have. And since we deal with other people (not just family, friends and colleagues, but neighbours, tutors, shop assistants, drivers and everyone else in the world) all the time, it's also incredibly handy to know how they're likely to react emotionally in any given situation.

Let's go back to anger, which started this chapter. Sometimes anger starts as a low-lying, slow-burning sense of frustration which, if not dealt with effectively, can build up over time like the steam in a pressure cooker, then suddenly explode, leading to actions which may be harmful to oneself as well as others. The emotionally intelligent person

This type of belief ↓	leads to	this emotion ↓	which leads to	this type of behaviour ↓
My rights have been violated in some way or I have been trespassed against	↑	Anger	↑	Attacking or lashing out
I have lost something	↑	Sadness	↑	Withdrawing or disengaging
I'm in danger	↑	Fear	↑	Running away
↓	↓	↓	↓	Or you can start here and work backwards

recognizes their own frustration as it occurs, understands how it develops and takes steps to defuse it before it gets out of hand.

A less obvious example of EI at work can be seen in good sales people. Not only do they intuitively understand which emotions their customer is currently experiencing, but they also anticipate how they will feel in certain situations, and use this knowledge to decide how best to clinch a deal.

 Have another look at your PANAS or SPANE results (see page 101) or think of a time recently when you became very aware of your own emotions. Perhaps you were elated, sad, or angry, or felt a combination of emotions.

What led you to feel this way? Can you identify your underlying thoughts and beliefs?

Was there a progression of different emotions, or a sudden switch from one emotion to another?

What patterns of emotional reaction do you recognize in yourself generally? What are your emotional triggers?

Try this exercise with a partner or friend.

The final attribute of an emotionally intelligent person is that he or she is able to **manage their emotions effectively**, for example, they know how to improve a bad mood, relax when they feel nervous, or remain calm when they're angry. Positive psychology research provides many insights into ways to regulate your emotions and change your mood from negative to neutral or positive. These include mindfulness (see Chapter 13), building hope and optimism (see Chapter 17) and developing resilience (see Chapter 19).

 Think forwards to a situation in which your emotions would typically be heightened, such as having to make a public speech or a presentation to a group of strangers. How would you like to feel as you're standing in front of them? And beforehand? What about afterwards? How might you achieve the most appropriate blend of emotions to ensure you give a polished performance?

All of us suffer from bad moods from time to time. EI experts suggest that the most successful mood regulation strategies involve expending energy. What strategies do you typically employ to change a bad mood, and how successful are they?

Here are some suggestions for managing your emotions and improving a bad mood:

- Expend some energy – try a brief burst of physical exercise, say 10 or 20 minutes. Even a quick walk up the road and back can lift your spirits.
- Change position – stand up, look up, stretch your whole body and walk around. Go outside if you can.

- Avoid drink, drugs and comfort food – these are short-term mood-enhancers which merely sap your self-control and lead to other issues in the long run.
- Listen to your favourite relaxing or uplifting music.
- Meditate or try 5 minutes of mindfulness – see Chapter 13 for some suggestions.
- Find a pleasant distraction or do a good deed – spend half an hour on your favourite hobby, run an errand for a neighbour or get the coffee in for your colleagues at work.
- Reframe the situation in a more positive way.
- Phone a good friend – a problem shared is often a problem halved.

How to manage others' emotions:

- Listen attentively
- Ask questions sensitively
- Acknowledge the emotion(s) they are feeling.

- Emotional intelligence is not just about understanding and managing your own emotions, it's about understanding and managing other people's too.

- In the workplace, people who have higher EI ratings are judged to be better at persuading, generating enthusiasm for their ideas and group decision-making. They also have higher ratings of job performance from their bosses, bigger merit increases, a higher rank in the company, and other people think they have greater leadership potential.

- There is no doubt that being self-aware, empathic, self-controlled and socially-skilled is an advantage, but claims that in the work-place EI is *more* important than IQ are difficult to prove.

- There is a view held by eminent researchers that developing your EI is not a quick fix but a life-long process of learning to navigate new relationships and situations, in which you hone your social skills as you go. So, if you feel your emotional intelligence is on the low side, do not despair – it can be learned!

12. Gratitude

When was the last time you said 'thank you' to someone and really meant it? Today? Earlier this week perhaps? Last month? And when was the last time you wrote a thank you card? That's probably a little more difficult to answer. As a child, you can no doubt remember your parents making you write thank you letters to Aunty and Uncle so-and-so for the birthday or Christmas gifts, but as adults we seem to get out of the habit of thanking people formally.

And yet there is increasing psychological evidence that grateful people are more attentive, determined, energetic, enthusiastic, helpful, interested, joyful and optimistic than those who aren't. On top of that, recent research suggests that gratitude is strongly related to what psychologists call your 'sense of coherence', your belief that life is manageable, meaningful, and understandable. The reason gratitude has such a powerful and lasting effect on your well-being is that it helps you reframe your experiences in a positive way.[20]

If that's not enough to persuade you to get out your pen and start writing your thank you letters, research also indicates that people who have a grateful disposition are less anxious, depressed, envious, lonely and materialistic. It turns out that gratitude is one of the top five character strengths consistently and robustly associated with life satisfaction (the others being zest, love, hope and curiosity).

If you want to develop an 'attitude of gratitude', why not try some of the following activities?

1. Keep a gratitude journal

Get hold of an attractive blank notebook or journal – this will become your gratitude journal. If you prefer to do everything electronically, simply create a new file on your PC or smartphone (although this may be a less flexible option in the long run). At the end of every week, give yourself 15 minutes and find somewhere comfortable to sit back and relax. Think back over the past seven days and write down all the things that you are thankful for. These don't have to be earth-shattering events or experiences; being grateful that you remembered your brolly on the day of the torrential rain, that your baby niece recovered quickly from chickenpox, or that your car passed its MOT are all absolutely fine.

As the weeks and months pass, you will find that your outlook shifts – you will start looking at life more positively, and your attention will be drawn away from the negative aspects of living towards the things that go right. This is an important part of increasing your well-being because it counteracts that in-built negativity bias that we humans have evolved.

And on top of this, you'll benefit from having a beautiful and growing record of positive life moments to reflect on, should you feel down and in need of a pick-me-up at any point.

CASE STUDY

My colleague Miriam regularly writes a gratitude journal. Here's what she says about it:

'Keeping a gratitude journal has changed my mindset from one of deprivation, where I was aware of all that was lacking in my life, to one of abundance. I am so much more aware now of all the good things that happen, because I keep a note of them in my journal. It's like you get another taste of the good times. A chance to savour those positive memories all over again.'

Some people suggest you should write every day, but if this becomes a chore, you may lose the motivation to keep it up. To increase the chance that you will actually stick to writing your gratitude journal, I suggest writing once a week.

2. Write a thank you card or letter

Writing a thank you card or letter is a simple way of acknowledging and appreciating what other people have done for you. When was the last time you actually received a thank you card or letter from someone? When I did a poll of my friends and colleagues recently, the answer was surprisingly few, although those who had received one really appreciated it. 'It brings a smile to my face every time I look at it', said Anish. 'I kept mine on the mantelpiece for weeks,' said Mel, 'and eventually stuck it on the fridge door.' So, it's not just the person who says thanks who benefits, it's also the person on the receiving end.

Think of someone who has done something for you, it doesn't matter how small. Perhaps you'd like to thank a neighbour for inviting you round for drinks on New Year's Eve. It could be that you're really grateful to a teacher who inspired your love of acting and who persuaded you to try for drama school when everyone else was dead set against it. Maybe you'd like to thank your boss or a colleague for helping you with a particularly tricky project at work.

Reflect on what this person has done which you're really grateful for. Write your card or letter, describing specifically what they did and what influence it had on you. It can be as long or as short as you like. You don't actually have to send the card or letter in order to benefit from feeling grateful, but if you want the other person to also feel good, then pop it in the post or deliver it personally.

3. Three good things

At the end of the day, think about the three good things that went well for you that day. These can be significant things or small things, it really doesn't matter.

You might like to share your three good things with a partner, but you don't have to, it's up to you. Research suggests that doing this activity daily will improve your well-being over the longer term.

It's also worth saying that this exercise is a great one to try with young children: it's a good way to instil a 'habit of happiness'.

My friend Stefan has an eight-year-old daughter who sometimes finds it difficult to get to sleep. Her mind is on the go the whole time, and when she's tired, she can get a little anxious or pessimistic about things.

One thing he has found which really helps is to ask Lotti to tell him her three good things when he tucks her up in bed. That way, her mind is focused on something positive. 'It's great to see her with a smile on her face last thing', Stefan said, 'and it helps her relax more so that she's ready for sleeping.'

4. WWW: what went well?

Psychologists suggest that the human brain has evolved over thousands of years to focus first and foremost on the negative side of life. In the Stone Age we wouldn't have survived as a species if we hadn't had the capacity to anticipate a sabre-toothed tiger over every hill top.

Whilst nowadays, especially in the developed world, there are few survival risks of this magnitude for us to contend with, it is taking time for our brains to learn this and rewire themselves. In the meantime, psychologists suggest that we've become conditioned to think negatively, so we have to make a conscious effort to turn our minds to the positive.

An exercise called 'What went well?' is a great way to start the process of putting positive things first. It works by simply focusing you on the things that worked, what you can learn from them, and what you can build on next time.

'What went well?' is a particularly useful technique to try in work situations as an antidote to the usual end of project 'post-mortem' when the team discusses what went wrong and what needs to be put right next time.

- Feeling grateful is correlated with life satisfaction: the higher your gratitude, the happier you'll feel, and vice versa.

- Making a habit out of gratitude is simple to do. As with many positive psychology techniques, the more you practise, the easier it becomes.

- You'll also improve other people's well-being by expressing your thanks to them. Everyone likes to feel appreciated.

- Even if you feel there is nothing big in your life to be grateful for, there will be many small things. If in doubt, seek inspiration from one of the online gratitude journals.

- Over time your attention will turn more easily to the positive side of life, so persevere!

- You can use your gratitude journal as a source of inspiration and comfort when you are feeling down.

---

13. Mindfulness

The practice of meditation is thousands of years old yet it's only relatively recently that it has been the subject of scientific research to investigate its benefits. Often meditation is associated with Eastern spiritual practice or new-ageism, and is easily dismissed as irrelevant by those of a more secular persuasion. Hopefully this chapter will dispel any doubts you may have about meditation, its importance, and in particular its benefits for your health and well-being.

Common misconceptions include thinking meditation is

- About escaping from reality or going into a trance
- Something which only Buddhist monks do
- About concentrating or thinking hard about something, or conversely, an absence of thinking
- Only appropriate for spiritual, religious or new-age people.

Mindfulness is a specific type of meditation-based practice which has been gaining in popularity in the Western world over the past 30 or so years. The name perhaps most associated with mindfulness meditation is Jon Kabat-Zinn, Professor of Medicine emeritus and founding director of the Stress Reduction Clinic and the Center for Mindfulness in Medicine, Health Care and Society at the University of Massachusetts Medical School.

Kabat-Zinn defines mindfulness as paying attention in a particular way: on purpose, in the present moment and non-judgementally. Put simply, it's about being able to tune in to what is happening in and around us in a conscious and purposeful way.

One way to understand mindfulness is to think about its opposite, mindlessness. Mindlessness is about doing things automatically, unconsciously, habitually, without awareness or oblivious to what is happening in and around you. When you stop to think about it, I'm absolutely certain that you will have experienced many moments in which you've 'lived mindlessly', that is, where you've gone on to autopilot and done things automatically, without awareness. A great example is eating. Often we eat without thinking about what we're doing, without noticing how the food feels or tastes in our mouths, and with no awareness of how full or not we're feeling before, during or after eating. I'm sure I'm not the only one who has been so busy talking that I've cleared my plate without consciously tasting much of the food on it! Many of us now eat in front of the TV or while we're reading, walking or even driving, making it all the more difficult to notice the various physical sensations associated with eating. One of the exercises we'll practise below is about eating mindfully.

Five essential steps to mindfulness

1. Be non-judgemental or impartial
2. Accept things as they are
3. Notice thoughts and emotions as they occur
4. Be fully in the moment
5. Be observant.

Some people find the concept of mindfulness difficult to grasp, especially if they've spent their whole lives focusing on finishing tasks and achieving goals. Others feel guilty about trying to do something which has no obvious target; we're all so busy these days and few of us can afford to waste time. Fortunately, research suggests that there are many mental and physical benefits associated with practising mindfulness.

How mindfulness helps
Research links mindfulness meditation with a long list of personal and interpersonal benefits including:

- Better control of emotions
- Decreased rumination (dwelling on negative thoughts)
- Improved working memory
- Better self-awareness
- Improved awareness of thoughts

- Reduced depression and anxiety
- Reduced physical illness
- Decreased emotional reactivity
- More flexible thinking
- Increased positive emotion
- Decreased negative emotion

My colleague Andy, who has practised and been a trainer in mindfulness for over 10 years, says, 'The more I practise the more I feel that magic flows into the present moment and I become less distracted by nagging doubts. By training the mind to focus on what's in front of you, you become more aware of opportunities to help others and yourself and fully appreciate how precious life is'.

Now let's start our mindfulness practice with a couple of simple activities.

1. Eating mindfully

Take 5 minutes out of your normal schedule. Find a couple of small snacks or other edible treats, such as pretzels, small pieces of cereal, chocolate or raisins. You also need a quiet place to sit.

First of all, eat one of your chosen snacks in your normal fashion. Then pick up a second one and go through the following steps. Take your time, don't rush.

1. Start by looking carefully at it. Imagine that you have never seen a pretzel or a raisin before. Notice its

colour and texture, turn it over carefully and slowly in your hand. Notice how its colour changes as the light catches it. Notice the fine grains of salt on the pretzel, or the crinkles on the surface of the raisin. Sniff it. What odour can you detect? Imagine eating the pretzel or raisin, imagine putting it in your mouth. Notice how your mouth starts to water at the mere thought of eating it. If at any point you start thinking 'Why am I doing this?' or 'This is a waste of time', acknowledge these as thoughts. Then return your attention to the object.

2. Having observed the snack closely from every angle, put it in your mouth but don't eat it just yet. What is the first sensation you notice? Is it taste or touch? How does the snack feel as you roll it around your mouth?

3. Now start to bite into or chew the snack. How does it feel when you bite into it for the first time? Do you get a satisfying crunch, or a soft chewy sensation? Notice the taste – is it a single flavour or a combination? Is it salty, sweet or both? Take your time, imagining that you must make it last forever.

4. Finally, swallow, noticing any aftertaste or other sensations in your mouth.

5. Having eaten the snack, how do you feel? How did it feel to eat the snack mindfully?

Now compare this with your experience of eating the first snack. Often, the first time people eat mindfully, they cannot believe how different it is to their normal experience of eating and how much enjoyment can be squeezed out of one tiny piece of food. You can do the same thing with drinking – a small glass of your favourite beer, wine or fruit juice will be just as effective for starting your mindfulness practice.

2. Sitting mindfully

Find yourself a comfortable place to sit and relax for 5 minutes. If at any point your mind wanders (it is very likely to), acknowledge your thoughts and return your attention calmly and without judgment to the exercise.

1. Rest your hands loosely on your lap. Plant your feet firmly on the ground and sit forward, don't slouch. Tuck your chin in slightly. Take a couple of deep breaths in through your nose and out through your mouth, then shut your eyes. Notice how the chair, bench or log you're sitting on feels underneath you. How do your legs and feet feel?

2. As you sit with your eyes closed, notice the sounds around you. What can you hear? A ticking clock? The distant noise of traffic? Rain on the window? Birdsong? The hum of the fridge? A dog barking? Silence? Pay attention to whatever you can hear, noticing the quality, pace and tone of the sounds as they come and go.

3. As you sit with your eyes closed, notice any smells – perhaps it's your own perfume or aftershave you notice first; or the smell of mown grass or cut flowers in a vase;

or the waft of cooking or baking from your kitchen; or the whiff of cigarette smoke from a passer-by. Register all the different smells.

4. Notice how your body feels as you sit there. Do you feel warm or cool? If outside, can you feel a breeze or the sunshine on your face? Are you completely relaxed or is there any tenseness in your body, perhaps in your shoulders, neck or back? If so, shake it or stretch it out. How do you feel? What mood are you in? Just notice, without judging.

5. Finally, notice your breathing (we will do a fuller breathing exercise next). Breathe through your nose. Notice how your breath makes your chest or stomach rise and fall. After a few moments of complete relaxation, take a deep breath, stand up, stretch your body and open your eyes.

Even though you were sitting for 5 minutes at the most, it may have felt like a lot longer. This is one of the unusual features of mindfulness; when you really pay attention to something (it could be eating, breathing, seeing, listening or anything really), it's as if time slows down.

3. Mindful breathing
If this is the first time you have tried a mindful breathing exercise, allow yourself no longer than 5 minutes. If you can, set an alarm or a timer to remind you when the time is up.

1. Find a place where you won't be disturbed. Sit comfortably, placing your hands loosely in your lap, and plant your feet firmly on the ground. Sit forward a little, keep your back straight and tuck your chin in slightly.
2. Take a couple of deep breaths in through your nose and out through your mouth, then shut your eyes. Notice how the chair you're sitting on feels underneath you. How do your legs and feet feel? Notice any other sensations in the body. Are you warm or cool? What can you hear around you? Acknowledge any sounds. Scan your whole body from top to toe, noticing any areas of tension or relaxation.
3. Now turn your attention to your breath. Breathing normally, notice how each breath feels as it flows in and out. What rising and falling sensations does the breath create? Can you feel it in your chest, stomach, shoulders or somewhere else?
4. Slowly begin to count, 1 as you inhale, 2 as you exhale, 3 as you inhale, 4 as you exhale and so on, all the way up to 10, before starting from 1 again. Do this silently.
5. You will notice as you do this that you may become distracted by thoughts as they pop up in your mind. This is perfectly normal. Simply acknowledge the thought and gently bring your awareness back to your breath. Start counting again.
6. Repeat steps 4–5 until the 5 minutes are over.
7. Sit quietly for a few moments longer. Thoughts may rush into your mind at this point, or you may feel calm.

8. Slowly return your attention to how you feel sitting there and when you are ready, open your eyes.

Mindful breathing is at the heart of mindfulness meditation. The point is to notice your thoughts as if from a distance, without getting caught up in what they are about. Mindful breathing is a simple technique, which you can practise pretty much anywhere, but it can be quite hard to begin with. As my mindfulness tutors Terry and Marianne say, you don't have to enjoy mindfulness practice, you just have to do it. So keep trying!

- Mindfulness has huge benefits for both your psychological and physical health.

- Many day-to-day activities can be done mindfully, so why not make up your own exercises?

- Mindful breathing is a quick yet very effective technique, although it takes practice.

- You don't have to enjoy mindfulness to benefit from it – you just need to keep practising.

- Don't worry if you find mindfulness hard at first – keep trying.

14. Mindsets

The theory of mindsets and their relevance to your performance, motivation and well-being have been the subject of study for the Stanford University academic and psychology researcher, Carol Dweck, since the 1970s. Put simply there are two mindsets: if you have a **fixed mindset** you believe that your personal qualities (such as intelligence) or abilities (such as musical talent or sporting prowess) are carved in stone, whereas if you have a **growth mindset** you believe that your personal qualities and abilities can be changed or developed over time.

What is particularly important about Carol Dweck's research for us as individuals is that it demonstrates how mindsets can have a significant impact on our behaviour and the way we live our lives.

How your mindset affects your behaviour
There are a number of ways that your mindset affects your behaviour, some of which may surprise you.

Our mindset influences:

- The kind of goals we pursue
- How we respond to failure and whether we stick at something or give up easily
- How much effort we make to achieve an ambition
- Whether or not we try new solutions when problems crop up.

We will now look at each of these in turn.

1. Goals – is it the journey or the destination which matters?

Carol Dweck suggests that people with a fixed mindset decide on 'performance goals'. For a student, this might mean passing an exam or achieving a certain grade or percentage in an assignment. For a sportsman, this might mean skiing down the black run this winter holiday. For a saleswoman, this might mean selling a certain volume or value of goods in a month. In this way, a person's qualities or ability can be measured easily, since either they meet their set performance target, or they don't. Meeting the set criteria means that their skill or ability is validated. The reverse is also true. If they fall short of the set target, for example getting a B rather than an A in an exam, it means that they aren't clever after all. You could say that a fixed mindset is a kind of black and white thinking – either you're capable, clever and talented, or you're not.

On the other hand, people with a growth mindset aren't so hung up on their performance; they're more inter-ested in setting 'learning goals' which means that they're focused on gaining competence in an area first, and then mastering it. For them, life is less about winning and losing, or passing and failing, and more about growing and learn-ing from everything they do. It may be helpful for you to think about fixed and growth mindsets using a travel meta-phor – growth mindset people set out with the intention of thoroughly enjoying and getting the most from the journey, whereas fixed mindset people are more concerned about reaching their destination.

THINK ABOUT IT

For a fixed mindset person, it isn't just failure which is upsetting. Ironically, even achieving your performance goal can cause anxiety. This is because once you've achieved your goal you have to keep performing at this level (or higher) in order to maintain the belief that you are clever, able, gifted or worthy. Falling below the standard shakes your belief in yourself and your ability to the core, and this creates additional pressure on you to keep performing at a higher and higher level.

With a fixed mindset you really can't win!

---

2. Responding to failure

Dweck's research suggests that fixed mindset people who fail to achieve their performance goals then feel helpless and hopeless. In a college assignment, for example, students with a fixed mindset focus solely on the grade; they pay little attention to the information which might help them learn and improve their performance next time round, and their teacher's or tutor's notes get ignored. If the grade is lower than they hoped or expected, they quickly get depressed, lose self-confidence and run out of steam. Their response has a sense of permanence about it. For example, failing an exam, or not getting the required grade, simply means that they're stupid. Full stop. According to Dweck, those with a fixed mindset are likely to say: 'I'll never be able to do it, so I won't bother trying again.'

For growth mindset people, failure isn't such a big deal. Rather than focusing on how they feel, growth mindset people focus on what they can learn from the experience which will help them do better next time, and they're more willing to try new approaches in order to improve. They believe that doing badly in an exam doesn't mean they're stupid; it's just a reflection of how they're doing at this point in time. They're more likely to say: 'It's beyond me, for now.'

3. Making an effort

 Answer the following question:

When you think about intelligence, how much is about the effort you make and how much is about your ability?

Intelligence = _____ per cent effort
+ _____ per cent ability

In research, fixed mindset people typically say that intelligence is 35 per cent effort and 65 per cent ability, whereas growth mindset people say that it's 65 per cent effort and 35 per cent ability.

What did you say?

Fixed mindset people believe that effort reflects lower intelligence and believe 'If I have to work hard it must mean that I'm not clever'. On the other hand, growth mindset people see effort in terms of greater success, so the harder they work, the more likely they are to succeed. 'If at first you don't succeed, try, try again' and 'practice makes perfect' are mottos created by and for growth mindset people!

 Several years ago at a positive psychology conference, I had the pleasure of hearing the inspirational British swimmer Adrian Moorhouse talk about drive, persistence and goals. We wanted to know how he'd bounced back from poor performance in the 1984 Olympics, where he'd only managed 4th and 6th places, despite being predicted to do much better. His recipe for success was adopting a growth mindset. He didn't focus on beating his opponents' times (a performance goal) – what he was more interested in was improving his swimming performance and pool turns little by little, learning something new every day. In short he persisted. By doing this he was motivated to keep trying harder rather than allowing himself to become discouraged by hearing the news of a rival swimmer's progress.

And history shows that this strategy worked: in 1988, Moorhouse won Olympic gold in the 100m breaststroke.

Practice makes perfect?

Tony de Saulles, writer and illustrator of Horrible Science books, is passionate about spreading the word that practice is essential. 'Many children seem to think that you are either good at something or not', he told me recently, 'and I think it's quite exciting for them to hear that actually, you can become reasonably good at anything you want to be good at if you are prepared to practise'.

So persistence, or refusing to give up when faced with disappointment or discouragement, is essential for success. How often are overnight successes really overnight? Not very often! Research into expert performance suggests that 10,000 hours (or roughly 10 years) of deliberate practice is required in order to reach the top of your field, whether that's in sports, science or scrabble! For more on this topic, see Chapter 7.

Positive psychologists emphasize that persistence is one human strength which can be improved, simply by practising difficult and demanding tasks. Chris Peterson also suggests using your perseverance in new ways, such as making a list of things to do and doing one of them every day, or finishing an important task ahead of schedule.

4. Strategies

The final area in which fixed mindset and growth mindset people differ is in the behaviours they adopt when challenged. When faced with a problem, fixed mindset people typically keep repeating the same behaviour. Eventually they get the message that this doesn't work, but rather than try something new, they give up completely. Growth mindset people aren't so easily dissuaded. They think of problems as opportunities to try new strategies. So of course by doing this they're far more likely to be successful in the end.

How to change your mindset

One of the techniques that Carol Dweck uses to help people change from a fixed to a growth mindset is to teach them about basic brain functioning. We know, for example, that our brains form new neural connections when we learn new things, and that new connections cause the brain to grow (in density not size!) Studies show that the part of the brain which deals with 3D space is denser (it has more neural connections) in taxi-drivers than it is in non-taxi drivers. Musicians have a better developed auditory cortex than non-musicians. Evidence from neuroscience suggests that by learning or practising something new, you can 'develop' your brain. So, think of your brain as a muscle which needs exercise; the more practice it gets, the stronger it becomes.

Failing forward

Think of an occasion in the past when your mindset has worked against you and stopped you getting what you want. Be honest. Perhaps you set your sights on achieving something, and when you didn't, you gave up, pretending that the goal didn't matter after all.

What can you learn from your 'failure'? Knowing what you now know about fixed and growth mindsets, what would you do differently next time? Jot down your ideas in your well-being journal.

Growth mindset superhero

Think of someone close to you, a sibling, a friend or colleague, who displays a growth mindset – perhaps towards their career, their relationships or their study. Recall a time when they've overcome a difficult set-back or a series of obstacles.

Reflect on exactly what they did to rise above the problem and find a solution. What can you learn from their approach? Record your ideas in your well-being journal.

Developing a growth mindset in others

If you're a parent, have you ever referred to one of your children as 'the clever one' and another as 'the sporty (or arty) one'? Or perhaps you yourself were pigeon-holed in this way as a youngster. Unfortunately this type of labelling can help cement a fixed mindset in a child's mind.

As well as teaching basic brain functioning, we can also use praise to develop a growth mindset in others, especially children and young people. Studies have found that you can do this *by praising the effort they make instead of their intelligence or their ability*. So, eradicate 'what a clever boy/girl!' from your vocabulary now. This is especially important since most schools, with their fixation for achieving targets, only encourage a fixed mindset.

- A fixed mindset limits your opportunities.

- A growth mindset expands your horizons.

- If you have a fixed mindset, you can change it.

- Your brain grows in density the more you learn and practise new things.

- Your brain is like a muscle, so exercise it!

- Expert performance is the result of approximately 10,000 hours of deliberate, effortful practice.

- Praise children for their effort, not for their intelligence or ability.

---

15. Motivation and goals

Motivation and goal theory forms an important part of well-being research even though, like other concepts which are now accepted as part of a positive psychology approach, it's been around for many years. Broadly speaking there are two main types of motivation, intrinsic and extrinsic. If you're intrinsically motivated to do something it means that your motivation is internal and driven by your own interest or enjoyment. If you're extrinsically motivated it means that your motivation is external, that is, it's driven by external incentives and disincentives such as money, high grades, coercion, competition or fear of punishment.

There are a vast number of benefits associated with high self-motivation (i.e. being intrinsically motivated) such as:

- Greater confidence
- Improved vitality
- More interest
- Enhanced performance
- Increased persistence
- Greater creativity
- Higher self-esteem
- Increased general well-being

If you're working now or have worked in the past, you're very likely to be familiar with the practice of goal-setting, since it forms part of the annual business planning process in many organizations. Often the progress we make against the goals we've set dictates the size of our annual bonus. Even those of you who haven't worked in organizations which set goals in this way may have experience of creating personal goals (such as New Year's resolutions) that you can draw on.

Goals fall into two broad categories. The first kind are **approach goals** which are goals with positive outcomes which we work towards. 'Positive' can mean different things in different contexts, including liked, desirable, pleasurable and beneficial. An example of an approach goal could be to move to the countryside for the peace and quiet.

Avoidance goals, on the other hand, are goals with negative outcomes which we work to avoid. The word 'negative' can also mean different things in different contexts, including disliked, undesirable, painful and harmful. An avoidance goal could be to move out of the city because it's noisy and busy.

Experts in goal theory suggest that approach goals can make an essential contribution to our well-being: all of us need goals in our lives, firstly because making progress towards achieving a valued goal makes us feel good, and secondly because we get a sense of satisfaction from identifying and pursuing life goals which are consistent with our core values. Psychology research suggests that avoidance goals are stressful because constantly monitoring negative possibilities drains our energy and enjoyment, eventually taking its toll on our well-being. What's more, avoidance goals can only facilitate surviving because, even when they are successfully achieved, they can only ever lead to the *absence* of something negative. On the other hand if we set ourselves approach goals to work towards, our focus is on achieving the *presence* of something positive, which is more energizing and enjoyable. Psychologists say that this ultimately leads to greater well-being too.[21]

Think about the goals you have in your life at the moment, either at work or at home. Are they approach or avoidance goals? If the latter, how can you reframe them into approach goals? Write them down in your well-being journal. Ask a friend or partner to help if you get stuck.

According to psychologists Richard Ryan and Edward Deci's self-determination theory of human motivation and behaviour, it isn't the goal *per se* which is important for our self-motivation and well-being but whether in identifying and pursuing the goal, three basic human needs are met. These needs are easily remembered as follows:

- Control
- Competence
- Connection

Control

Control refers to autonomy, or the need to choose how we act. When your goal is your own choice, nobody is making you do it, and your decisions about what to do and how to do it are your own, then you are said to be 'acting autonomously'. Feeling that you have a choice about how you live your life makes an important contribution to your self-motivation and well-being.

Conversely, if you feel under pressure to think, feel and behave in a certain way (such as feeling that you're being coerced or doing something because you'll receive some kind of reward) then you're not acting autonomously, and your self-motivation and well-being will be decreased.

When you think about your current goals (work or personal), are they really freely chosen? Are you doing them to please yourself or to please someone else? If you decide that your goal is not your own choice, how might you change it so that you increase the amount of control you have? Record your reflections in your well-being journal.

Studies have repeatedly shown that giving external rewards in return for 'good' behaviour, such as offering performance-related pay at work or giving pocket money to children in return for doing homework, as well as meting out punishments for 'bad' behaviour, all undermine intrinsic motivation.

137

Competence

The second element of self-determination theory is **competence**. This refers to the human need to feel confident, effective and masterful in whatever we do.

When you think about your current goals and your progress towards them, do you receive regular positive and constructive feedback about how you are performing, and does the feedback you get inspire you to perform better? If not, how could you acquire such feedback? Think about the other ways in which you can improve your competence in relation to this goal. Perhaps you can look at different ways to improve your skill-set, such as practising for longer or undertaking further training. You might also like to revisit Chapter 14 at this point. Record your ideas in your well-being journal.

Connection

This is the third element of self-determination theory. It refers to the need in every human being to have relationships with other people which are both close and secure, while at the same time giving us the freedom to make our own choices (see Chapter 5).

When you think about your current goals, at home or at work, do you have positive support from the people around you? If not, how could you acquire it? Who could you approach who might be willing to assist, by giving you advice and guidance, for example? Who could coach or mentor you? Commit to acquiring the support you need within the next few days. Record your commitment in your well-being journal.

Ryan and Deci's self-determination theory suggests that when the basic needs for control, competence and connection are satisfied, our self-motivation and well-being will be enhanced. So, the important questions for you to consider are:

- How can you achieve more control, competence and connection in your life?
- How can you help other people achieve their goals by facilitating control, competence and connection for them?

Think forward to an important event or activity which is coming up in the next month. This can be related either to your personal life or to your work life.

Consider what you can do to increase the 3 Cs in relation to this event or activity.

CASE STUDY

My colleague Alex was asked to give a talk to a local youth group about positive parenting. By discussing it with his friends, neighbours and other parents at school, and inviting them and their teenage children to come along to support him, he improved the quantity and quality of his **connections**. As for **competence**, he spent extra time rehearsing what he was going to say and do, visited the venue in advance to get the lie of the land, and prepared a couple of additional activities in case there were any quiet moments to fill. That way he felt as well-prepared as he could be. Having researched the topic of his presentation and discussed various aspects of it with others, the amount of **control** he felt was increased by making his own decisions about what and how to present.

By finding ways to emphasize the 3Cs, you'll also increase your feeling of self-motivation, and you're more likely to gain a sense of achievement and satisfaction.

Self-control and commitment to your goals

I expect all of us can think of times when we started the New Year with a strong resolution to make an important change in our lives, only to find our self-motivation disappearing within a matter of days. What on earth went wrong?

TRY IT NOW!

Can you think of a goal towards which your progress is not as great as you would have liked by this stage?

On a scale of 1–10, where 0 means 'not at all committed' and 10 means 'absolutely committed', how committed are you to achieving this goal? Be honest!

If you score less than 10/10, ask yourself *what exactly would have to change* in order for you to score 10/10?

It may be that, on reflection, you feel that your goal is not solely within your control, you don't know where to start, or the way it's framed focuses on extrinsic elements.

How can you use what you now know about control, connection and competence to build your self-motivation? Record your ideas in your well-being journal.

Many coaches will tell you that the reason for not achieving a goal is because it wasn't SMART enough (we covered SMART goals in Chapter 4). The SMART model is frequently used in business to help the goal-setting process. A lot of coaches believe that making a goal SMART is pretty much a guarantee of success. If only it were that straightforward! Yes, the SMART attributes may help, but people's New Year's resolutions can falter for other reasons, such as a lack of self-control and commitment, or conflict with other goals.

If you think that poor self-control may be behind your lack of goal success, you are not alone! In a recent study of the various character strengths of over 17,000 adults in the

UK, self-control was found consistently near the bottom of the list.[22] On the plus side it was also found to increase with age, so there is hope for all of us!

Self-control, according to psychologist Roy Baumeister, is a bit like a muscle – the more you exercise it the stronger it gets. This means that being more disciplined in one domain of your life can help you develop greater self-control in other areas. At the same time, using self-control requires mental energy, so as with physical exercise, don't overdo it or you're more likely to lapse.

If self-control is not one of your strong points, you'll need to take baby steps at the start. As in any goal-setting exercise, give yourself a target to aim for, but don't set the bar so high that it's impossible to achieve. Doing that will simply demotivate you. Identifying the small steps which lead towards your ultimate goal is essential. If your aim is to run the marathon, you shouldn't start by trying to run the whole 26.2 miles on the first day of training. The key to self-control is to try to create new habits which simply become part of your day-to-day routine; after a while you don't need much self-control at all. Like cleaning your teeth morning and night, it becomes 'just something you do'.

Research from the field of neuroscience suggests that improving your working memory will help increase your self-control in all areas of your life.[23] You can improve your working memory using simple brain-training software such as the Dual N-Back game.

This is available online free from Sourceforge:

brainworkshop.sourceforge.net

Why not give it a go?

Looking to the future, or to the past?

Research into people's commitment to their goals suggests that it makes a difference to your self-motivation whether you focus on the progress you've already made towards your goal, or whether you focus on the things that you have left to achieve.

- If you are fully committed to your goal, you can maintain your self-motivation by focusing on **to go** information, that is, what you have left to accomplish
- But if your commitment is uncertain, you can increase your self-motivation by focusing on **to date** information, that is, what you have already accomplished.

Goals which are intrinsically motivating by definition need less self-control. Therefore if you can find ways to improve your self-motivation, you won't need to worry so much about your willpower.

Finally ...

Psychologist Sonja Lyubomirsky suggests that goals need to possess certain characteristics in order to enhance well-being. For example, goals which are intrinsic, congruent with your motives and needs, and not in conflict with each other, are more likely to enhance your happiness and life satisfaction. In short, not all goals are equal; certain goals enhance well-being whilst others do not.

- The satisfaction of three basic psychological needs (control, competence and connection) will increase your self-motivation, and your well-being.

- Improving your working memory will increase self-control in all areas of your life.

- If your commitment to your goal is uncertain, focus on what you have already achieved – this will help increase your self-motivation.

- If you are fully committed to your goal, focus on what you have left to achieve – this will help maintain high self-motivation.

- Self-control, which is essential for goal achievement, is like a muscle – the more you exercise it, the stronger it gets.

- How much willpower you have will be less of an issue if you're already highly motivated to do something.

- Not all goals are equal in the well-being stakes: make sure yours are intrinsic, congruent and in harmony with each other.

---

16. Nutrition

Food for thought

Nutrition, like physical exercise, is rather peripheral in positive psychology, which doesn't fully acknowledge that the human body is an integrated system. This means that food and diet is usually considered more relevant to physical health than to psychological health.

Although there still needs to be much more research linking nutrition to well-being and optimum functioning (the positives), there is growing empirical evidence which links what we eat to mental illnesses such as depression and behavioural problems such as ADHD and antisocial behaviour (the negatives). Whilst individual dietary advice can't be provided in this chapter, it's worth reviewing recent research and the basic rules of good nutrition.

A diet lacking certain vitamins, minerals and fatty acids such as fish-oil based omega-3 can lead to depression, anxiety, poor concentration and mood swings, as well as increased aggression. In one study, vitamins and other vital nutrients were added to the otherwise very poor diets of young offenders at a maximum security institution. Researchers found that those who received the supplements committed 25 per cent fewer disciplinary offences in custody than those who had been given a placebo. What's more, serious violent incidents in the prison were reduced by 40 per cent. Another study found that folic acid supplementation significantly improved the cognitive functions that decline with age. Although it is fair to say that scientific tests of individual nutrients often fail to show any positive effect, this may be because they need to be consumed in conjunction with others, as part of a balanced diet. This would explain why there *is* scientific evidence that the Mediterranean diet is associated with better cognition.

Poor physical health is often a sign that our eating habits need to be improved, and the same could be said of poor mental health. Many of us like to think that we eat healthily, but our memory can easily catch us out. When we record what we eat as we eat it, we're often surprised, not only by what we eat, but when and how much.

Food diary

Experts often recommend that people who are hoping to make changes in their lives start by keeping an activity record. By maintaining a simple food diary in your well-being journal over a couple of days you'll become much more aware of what you are eating, when, and how you feel about it. Once you have a good understanding of your eating habits, you'll be in a better position to makes some positive changes.

In your well-being journal, create a table with five columns as shown opposite.

Keep the food diary with you and fill it in for a couple of days. At the same time as recording what you eat and drink, it's helpful to make a note of where you were, and who you

Date/time	Food/drink consumed	Where	Who with	Thoughts/feelings at the time
e.g. 7.30 am	3 slices of white toast with butter and jam, 2 cups of black coffee	In the bedroom, whilst getting dressed and ready for work	Alone	Feeling rushed, didn't enjoy the food at all. Still felt hungry on the drive to the office.

were with, as well as what you were thinking and feeling at the time. This may help you to recognize certain triggers or patterns of behaviour, which you weren't previously unaware of.

If these eating patterns and habits aren't helpful, for example eating when you're not hungry, eating the wrong types of food, eating too much, eating when you're feeling stressed or anxious and so on, you can set goals to change them. Try to fill in the food diary as you go – this makes you more aware of what you're doing as you do it. It's also very easy to forget if you leave it till the end of the day. Whatever you do, make sure you're honest with yourself.

What is a healthy diet?

Diets like Atkins, GI or cabbage soup come and go, but one thing that hasn't changed much in the past few decades is advice about what constitutes a healthy diet.

A healthy diet should draw on all five major food groups:

- Starchy carbohydrates such as bread, rice, pasta, cereals and potatoes
- Fruit and vegetables
- Protein, for example from meat, fish and eggs
- Milk and dairy products
- Fat and sugar.

People are often told to have a 'balanced diet', but that doesn't mean consuming an equal quantity of each food group. The UK's National Health Service advises that your daily diet should consist of about one third carbohydrates and one third fruit and vegetables. The remaining third should be split between protein and milk and dairy products, with only a very small amount of your daily intake coming from fatty or sugary foods. Eating a balanced diet means that you're more likely to be getting all the essential vitamins and minerals without needing additional nutritional supplements. Before changing your diet, or if you're in doubt, you should speak to your GP or a registered dietician.

There are some vitamins and minerals which, when they're missing from your diet, can cause low mood and other psychological problems.

Mood-boosting vitamins and minerals

Folic acid is found in liver, green vegetables, oranges and other citrus fruits, beans and yeast extract. Folic acid deficiency is linked with fatigue, confusion and irritability.

Iron comes from red meat, dried fruit, lentils and most dark green leafy vegetables. Iron deficiency is linked to fatigue, irritability, apathy, inability to concentrate and increased depressive symptoms.

Omega-3 from fatty fish, such as mackerel, is essential to the development and function of the brain, but often lacking in the modern diet. Omega-3 deficiency is thought to contribute to the increased incidence of depression and anxiety as well as a wide range of developmental and psychiatric conditions, including dyslexia, attention deficit hyperactivity disorder (ADHD) and autism. Research suggests that omega-3 supplementation may have anti-depressant and mood-stabilizing effects. Note that plant-based omega-3 doesn't have the same benefits, so check the labels.

Vitamin B12 is found in meat, salmon, cod, milk, cheese, eggs and yeast extract. Severe vitamin B12 deficiency results in loss of memory, mental dysfunction and depression.

Vitamin C can be found in peppers, broccoli, Brussels sprouts, sweet potatoes, tomatoes, oranges and kiwi fruit. In small studies, high-dose vitamin C supplements have been shown to reduce major depression.

Selenium is present in Brazil nuts, fish, meat and eggs. Selenium is an important mood regulator; some studies have shown that selenium deficiency may increase depression and other negative moods.

Zinc is found in meat, shellfish, milk, dairy foods such as cheese, bread and cereal products such as wheatgerm. Depression is a common symptom of zinc deficiency.

If you do take food supplements, stick to the recommended dosage because some can be harmful if exceeded.

Processed foods

One of the contributors to a poor diet and mental health issues is the consumption of processed and refined foods. Researchers at University College London found that eating a diet high in processed food increases the risk of depression, whereas people eating plenty of vegetables, fruit and fish actually had a lower risk of depression.[24]

Other food and drink to avoid

To ensure that your diet is rich in vitamins and minerals, there are some foods and drinks which are best avoided, or consumed in small quantities.

1. **Alcohol**. Ironically, alcohol is a depressant, even though we often drink to make ourselves feel good. According to the Royal College of Psychiatrists, alcohol causes more harm than illegal drugs like heroin and cannabis. Many of us drink responsibly, but some of us don't.
2. **Caffeine**. Most people like their caffeine drinks for the buzz it gives them. What they probably don't know is that caffeine only works because you get a withdrawal effect when you don't drink it (such as overnight) which lowers alertness and mood, and decreases performance. Having another caffeine drink reverses these effects, but contrary to popular belief it doesn't actually boost functioning to above your 'normal' levels. Some studies suggest that it can also increase anxiety in susceptible individuals.
3. **Ready meals**. Whilst some of these may look healthy, don't be fooled by the labelling. Home-cooked food, free from preservatives and palate-pleasing added sugar, salt and fat, is usually a healthier option.

4. **Fast food**. Whilst some fast food outlets have improved the quality of their products, and offer healthy alternatives, this is not true of all of them.

5. **Crisps**. Did you know that the British eat more crisps and other savoury snacks per head than any other European country? Crisp consumption is estimated at 150 packets per person, per year. Crisps are full of hidden nasties such as fat, salt and sugar. Recently the British Heart Foundation campaigned to reduce the amount of crisps eaten by children because of the long-term health impact.

6. **Fizzy drinks**. Sugary soft drinks are bad for your teeth as well as your blood pressure and have been linked to the increase in obesity and type 2 diabetes.

7. **High glycaemic index (GI) foods.** These include white rice, many breakfast cereals and cakes. These foods will give you instant energy but it doesn't last, leaving you feeling hungry and very quickly searching for another snack.

A little home cooking

Have another look at your food diary. Can you tell roughly how much of your diet comes from processed and refined foods? Over the next week or so, try to alter the balance, so that you eat fewer pre-packaged foods and more raw fruit and vegetables and home-cooked foods. What difference do you notice in how you feel? Make notes in your well-being journal.

If you find this activity difficult, one great tip is to think ahead. Spend some time planning what you'll eat for each meal in the coming week, and ensure you have all the necessary ingredients by consulting cookery books or online recipes. Write a shopping list and stick to it when you do the supermarket shop or order online.

If you're not used to cooking at home, it's also a good idea to stick to quick and easy recipes first, to build up your confidence and skills. If you have kids, involve them in meal planning, shopping, food preparation and cooking. Even simple foods can taste fabulous when they're homemade and you'll soon be able to ditch the microwavable foods altogether and give Jamie Oliver a run for his money!

Having fun with food

As well as eating, there are plenty of other ways to enjoy food. You could organize a meal with a difference for a small group of friends. Share the cost and the fun of preparation by asking each guest to contribute one dish – a starter, an accompaniment to the main course or a pudding. Having an overall regional theme, like Mexican, Greek or Indian will ensure that you end up with a table laden with complementary foods, rather than an ill-matched assortment.

Or why not organize a 'safari supper' with some of your neighbours, where each course is prepared and eaten in a different house. Again, agreeing a food theme may help ensure that foods are agreeably co-ordinated, although you may prefer the surprise factor. This is also a fabulous way to get to know your neighbours better and build your social connections.

A third activity you can try in order to squeeze the maximum pleasure out of eating (or drinking) is to savour. For more information, research and activities related to savouring, see Chapter 20.

If you enjoy food, you might also explore the Slow Food movement, which promotes a greater enjoyment of food through a better understanding of its taste, quality and production.

Thinking about the human body as an interconnected system means that we need to take into account the impact of what we eat on how we think and how we behave. Food is a fuel, not just for the body, but for the mind as well.

THINGS TO REMEMBER!

- Follow the guidelines from nutrition experts and eat a balanced diet. This will help maintain your physical and mental fitness.
- If on reflection you believe you need nutritional supplements, consult your GP or a registered dietician. Always stick to the recommended dosage.
- There are plenty of ways to have fun with food, from cooking and eating with friends and neighbours to savouring and Slow Food.
- Whilst more scientific research is needed on the links between what we eat and drink and our mental health and well-being, there is sufficient evidence already to give us food for thought!

---

17. Optimism

Are you a glass half-full or a glass half-empty person? If you're a pessimist through and through, does it really matter? And if it does, can you do anything to change it?

Positive psychology sometimes gets criticized for being only about positive thinking. As you'll know from reading the other chapters in the book, there's far more to it than that. Nevertheless, is the ability to 'think positively' a good thing? Firstly let's look at the research. It turns out that whilst there are some downsides to being an optimist, they seem to be outweighed significantly by the benefits, which are both physical and psychological. In fact there are so many desirable characteristics linked to optimism that positive psychologist Chris Peterson dubbed it the 'Velcro construct' – everything sticks to it!

Benefits of optimism
- Optimists suffer less anxiety, depression and distress than pessimists
- Optimism is linked to more effective coping – optimistic people tend to deal with problems rather than avoid them and use more acceptance, humour and positive reframing
- Optimism is associated with higher life satisfaction and increased well-being
- Optimists have stronger immune systems and a lower cardiac risk

- Optimists recover from surgery more quickly and report a higher quality of life afterwards
- Optimists adapt better to negative events in their lives, such as serious illness
- Contrary to what you might think, optimists don't stick their heads in the sand by, for example, ignoring the warning signs of illness
- Optimists don't give up easily even when faced with serious adversity, whereas pessimists are more likely to anticipate disaster and give up as a result
- Optimists are more action-oriented when faced with problems, and more likely to accept the reality of a bad situation than pessimists.

Now that we've established some of the many good points about being optimistic, can pessimists learn how to become more optimistic? Well, the answer from positive psychologists such as Martin Seligman is an unequivocal yes. But the important thing is that it's less about thinking positively and more about thinking **flexibly and accurately** – in other words, learning to challenge unhelpful or negative ways of thinking which keep us stuck and unable to move on. So how can we become more flexible and accurate thinkers?

It's definitely not about repeating positive affirmations. These probably won't do you any harm (apart from wasting time), but they won't do much good either. Scientific research points to other, more practical strategies which have been shown to make a difference to people in real life, for example, reducing the risk of depression. Before we take a look at them, let's see how optimistic and pessimistic thinking operate in practice.

Explanatory or attributional style

One way of looking at optimism and pessimism is as different **explanatory styles**. An explanatory style means the way we explain our experiences or the events which happen to us. Research has found that optimists and pessimists have different explanatory styles. Optimists attribute the cause of negative events and experiences to external, specific and transient factors, whereas pessimists do the opposite; they attribute their cause to internal, global and permanent factors. Before we look at a detailed example, try the following activity.

 Think of a negative event or experience you've had in your life, preferably something from which you've now bounced back. Spend 5 minutes writing down your explanation of what happened, and why, in your well-being journal.

Now look at the example in the table overleaf. Can you identify your explanatory style?

Interestingly, these positions are reversed when we explain good events and experiences. Optimists think about them as being personal, permanent and pervasive, whereas pessimists think the opposite (see table on page 159).

Negative event: explaining why I didn't get that job

	Olivia the optimist says …	Pete the pessimist says …
Is it personal?	It's not my fault I was late for the interview, the traffic was terrible. Subtext: *No, it wasn't about me.*	I was stupid to take the car, I should have taken the train. Subtext: *Yes, it was about me.*
Is it permanent?	It was a one-off and I'll be fine at the next interview. Subtext: *No, it's transient, things can change.*	I'm never going to get a job. Subtext: *Yes, it's permanent, things are always going to be like this.*
Is it pervasive?	OK so I didn't get the job but that's not going to stop me enjoying my weekend away. Subtext: *No, it only affects a very specific part of my life.*	Not getting this job means the end of all my dreams. Subtext: *Yes, this affects everything about my life.*

Positive event: explaining why I got that job

	Olivia the optimist says …	Pete the pessimist says …
Is it personal?	I answered those interview questions brilliantly! Subtext: *Yes, it was down to me.*	They asked me the right questions in the interview. Subtext: *No, it wasn't about me at all.*
Is it permanent?	I got the job because I'm always well-prepared. Subtext: *Yes, things will always be like this.*	I was just lucky on the day. Subtext: *No, things won't stay this way.*
Is it pervasive?	I'm a very talented person. Subtext: *Yes, there's a global explanation which reflects well on the rest of my life.*	I said the right things in the interview. Subtext: *No, there's a very specific explanation which doesn't apply to other parts of my life.*

So, now that we have a good understanding of how optimists and pessimists think, and have identified our own explanatory style, how do we go about learning to be more optimistic?

The art of disputing

If you're prone to thinking the worst about yourself, other people and the world in general, maybe now's the time to consider changing. One very effective way of becoming more optimistic is to monitor your explanatory style and challenge the negative explanations you make. Psychologists call this **disputing**.

Take your negative story from the activity on page 157. Try to look at it again with a fresh pair of eyes. How else might the event or experience be interpreted? There are many ways of disputing negative beliefs.

 Ask yourself the following:

1a. What is the *evidence* for your negative explanation or belief?
1b. What *counter-evidence* can you think of that suggests it isn't true?

It'll be very easy to think of evidence which supports your initial explanation, and more difficult to think of evidence against. Persevere, and if needs be, ask a friend or colleague to help you.

2. Brainstorm as many *alternative more positive explanations* for this event or experience as you can think of. Set yourself a challenge to think of 3, 5 or even 10. It may help you to think in terms of external, temporary and specific causes. Don't allow yourself to be side-tracked into justifying why these alternatives aren't true.

Again, ask for support from a friend or colleague if you get stuck.

3. Now think about the *implications* of the negative event or experience. Firstly identify and describe the *worst* thing that could possibly happen as a result. Ask yourself how likely this is on a scale of 1–10. Secondly, identify and describe the *best* thing that could possibly happen. Finally, ask yourself what is the *most likely* thing to happen. By looking at the problem from all angles, you will arrive at a more realistic explanation of the event in question.

At this point it's worth stressing that you need to use your common sense, since there are situations where optimistic thinking should never be used. If the worst that could happen really *is* a disaster, do not ignore it. For example, do not be optimistic about needing to get the brakes repaired on your car.

4. Now consider which of these explanations or beliefs from steps 2 and 3 is *most useful* to you in terms of keeping you motivated, achieving your goals, and creating and maintaining good mood.

Reflect on how an alternative, more optimistic explanation of the negative event energizes you and leaves you feeling much more upbeat.

5. Martin Seligman suggests one final, practical step in this transformation from negative to positive, more accurate thinking, which is to *make an action plan*, focusing on what you can do to improve the situation. This, he says, is essential in order to avoid feelings of helplessness and to get you back in the driver's seat.

After you have worked through steps 1–5 above, take a further ten minutes to make an action plan, writing notes in your well-being journal.

But is optimism always good and pessimism always bad?

Research has found that there is a type of pessimist who doesn't benefit from learning how to be optimistic and being in a positive mood. This person is called the 'defensive pessimist'. Defensive pessimists use the expectation that things will turn out badly as a coping mechanism: they perform better when they're allowed to imagine what could go wrong and keep hold of their low expectations. Defensive pessimism helps anxious people manage their anxiety, and contrary to what you might think, trying to be optimistic actually makes their performance worse.

THINGS TO REMEMBER!

- There are a great many physical and emotional benefits associated with being optimistic.

- Learning optimism is about learning to think flexibly and accurately.

- Pessimists can learn to become more optimistic, for example by challenging negative trains of thought.

- You can reduce the risk of depression by learning optimism.

- When challenging negative thinking, if the worst thing that could happen really *is* a catastrophe, don't ignore it.

- Defensive pessimists, though, are better off continuing to expect the worst because this helps them manage their anxiety.

18. Physical exercise

Not exercising is like taking depressants.

Tal Ben-Shahar

Many of us give up the habit of doing regular physical exercise after we leave school or college, and rarely give it a second thought unless we're trying to lose weight. Even though the connection between a healthy mind and a healthy body has been made since ancient times, the benefits of physical exercise for psychological health have often been overlooked. Now there is growing interest in the scientific community about the link between physical and mental fitness, as well as empirical evidence pointing towards the many mental health benefits of regular exercise.

Probably the best known research on this topic is a study into the link between exercise and depression.[25] The research participants, who were all suffering from depression, were divided into three groups. The first group was prescribed anti-depressants, the second aerobic exercise, and the third a combination of anti-depressants and exercise.

Four months later, for the majority of participants their depression had improved. But the real surprise was that after 10 months, 38 per cent of those in the anti-depressants group and 31 per cent from the combination group (anti-depressants plus exercise) had relapsed, whereas only 9 per cent of those who did exercise alone became depressed again. These results suggest that physical exercise is a very powerful way to deal with certain mental illnesses and to maintain good mental health.

 Ideally, exercise needs to be fun and varied to keep you motivated – jogging the same route every few days will soon become tedious and your motivation will plummet.

- Find different forms of exercise that you enjoy and try to alternate them
- Consider a mix of individual, partner and team exercise – swimming, jogging, cycling and dancing call be done individually, with a buddy or as part of a team
- Look online to see what local clubs are near you. If your self-control isn't strong, being part of a group can help to increase your commitment and motivation
- Think outside the box. A 30-minute rapid walk with the dog every day will be just as good as a formal exercise regime. So will playing football with your kids in the park regularly. You don't have to choose a traditional form of exercise like swimming or squash. Anything which raises your heartbeat, such as Zumba, skipping or dry-slope skiing, can improve your physical fitness.

Benefits of physical exercise

Of course, lack of exercise is a factor in the obesity epidemic in many parts of the world. Obesity carries with it numerous physical health issues, as well as contributing to lower mood. In the UK in 2007 a government commissioned study predicted that if no action was taken, 60 per cent of men, 50 per cent of women and 25 per cent of children would be obese by the year 2050. Exercise is important for a healthy heart, reducing high blood pressure, maintaining a healthy weight and developing strong bones and muscles. Recent research suggests that aerobic exercise helps to create new brain cells (neurogenesis) in the areas of the brain which are known to shrink when people have mood problems. This is the case even in older adults; a recent study suggests that mental well-being in later life can be improved through exercise and physical activity. In 2005 a research team at the University of Illinois found that elderly people (average age 67) who were physically active also had more active brains, better mental skills and better memory than those who weren't physically active. Researchers then divided a group of elderly people into two groups, one which participated in an aerobic exercise programme, and one which didn't. They found that those who exercised increased their brain density compared with those who didn't.

Apart from helping create new brain cells, can physical exercise help us in other ways? Psychology research suggests that it is also linked to:

- Enhanced body image, self-esteem and self-perceptions
- Improved sleep patterns
- Reduced emotional distress and increased well-being

- Reduced depression
- Reduced stress
- Increased general health.

In one study, as little as 5 minutes a day of light resistance training (such as knee extensions and flexions using air resistance equipment) resulted in an increase in the subjective physical well-being of office-workers. Additionally there is evidence that physical exercise becomes more rewarding over time and reinforces positive feelings, which leads to better mental well-being.

The many advantages associated with physical exercise mean that it's too important to leave out of any discussion about mental health, happiness and well-being. If you do nothing else with your spare time, at least devote some of it to physical exercise. And if you're very new to physical exercise, check your level of health and fitness with your GP first.

The invisible benefit?

So why do we dread putting on our jogging shoes or donning our swimsuit when we know that we'll feel so much better at the end? New research suggests that people significantly underestimate how much they'll enjoy a good workout. It doesn't seem to matter what sort of exercise it is either – the research looked at individual and team activities, including yoga, pilates, aerobic exercise and weight training. The reason we aren't good at forecasting our positive emotions is that we put more focus on the beginning of the workout, which typically feels more unpleasant, than we do on the middle or the end of it.

In order to overcome this hurdle and at the same time increase your intention to take more exercise, researchers suggest several ways of enhancing your expected enjoyment. The first is to increase the positivity of the very beginning of an exercise routine. So, perhaps if you have a range of different exercises in your workout, do the one you enjoy most first. Another idea to make the beginning of your routine feel more pleasant is to play your all-time favourite music at the start. The third suggestion is to focus your attention in detail on the enjoyment and satisfaction you'll feel in the middle and during the cool-down phase, to counteract the unpleasant emotions you feel at the beginning.

Increasing your will-power

At this point it's worth mentioning that a little self-discipline goes a long way when it comes to physical exercise. Remember that we talked about the importance of self-control in Chapter 2.

If you're one of those people who doesn't own a tracksuit and only wears trainers as a fashion statement, then you may be interested to hear that your willpower is itself a bit like a muscle – not only does it get stronger with practice, it can also be overused!

So, 'little and often' would seem to be the best way to start out if you're new to regular physical exercise and fear your self-control may not last as long as your energy drink. Establish an exercise goal which contains smallish, doable steps, rather than setting the bar too high. This way you'll be increasing your willpower as well as your muscle-power as you walk, swim or dance your way to happiness.

Self-control – more bang for your bucks

There is one other interesting characteristic of self-control which is relevant here, and that is that developing self-control in one domain of your life can help improve your self-control in other areas. In one study participants who performed a two-month programme of physical exercise (including weightlifting, resistance training, and aerobics) became more successful at reducing their cigarette smoking, use of alcohol, consumption of caffeine and junk food, impulsive spending and TV viewing, and they ate more healthily, studied more and even did more washing up. Whilst doing more physical exercise might explain the change to a healthier diet and lifestyle, no-one is suggesting that it'll also turn you into a paragon of domestic virtue. Researchers explain this result by suggesting that improving your self-regulation can be beneficial across the board.

So that's another good reason for creating a workable physical exercise routine and sticking to it!

Getting started

The four cheapest forms of exercise are walking, running, swimming and cycling. They're also easy to organize in that, by and large, you can do them when you want. You can also enjoy them alone, with a partner or even as part of a group. As with all exercise routines, if you are very overweight, have a history of health problems or are currently recovering from surgery, you should consult your GP first.

Walking is a great 'starter' activity if you are new to exercise and need to improve your initial level of physical fitness. It's low impact, but a brisk 'power walk' up and down hills will provide some aerobic exercise and improve your heart and lung functioning, as well as burning around 100 calories in 15–20 minutes. Walking can be easily incorporated into your daily routine, whether that's walking to the local newsagent, taking the kids to school or walking the dog. If you normally take public transport to work, get off one or two stops early and walk the rest of the way. If you work in an office, take the stairs rather than the lift. And try to incorporate a brisk walk into your lunch break.

Running (or jogging) is another easy and relatively cheap form of aerobic exercise, though running experts recommend you invest in a good pair of running shoes. Start with a warm up, such as walking at a brisk pace first before you run. If you've never run before, aim to run for about 10 minutes at a time, interspersed with brisk walking. Depending on speed and terrain, running burns between 300 and 600 calories per hour. If you get bored easily, run with a partner so that you can chat as you go, or take along your iPod and listen to your favourite music or a podcast as you run.

Swimming is a great form of exercise because it's low impact, so it doesn't put any stress on your joints, but at the same time it tones your whole body. If you swim fast enough it can also provide a good aerobic workout, as well as helping you burn around 300–500 calories per hour. One of the great benefits of swimming is that you can go at your own speed. Try swimming a couple of lengths against the clock before doing a few more at a leisurely pace. Record how many lengths you do each time you swim and aim to increase the number of lengths, or maintain the number and swim faster. Many municipal pools offer reductions for swimming off-peak so it needn't be an expensive outlay. Why not see if work colleagues fancy a splash during the lunch break – even 30 minutes of swimming can leave you feeling refreshed and full of vitality.

Cycling, like swimming, doesn't put any pressure on joints, so it's a very good form of exercise for those with joint problems. Cycling at a pace which leaves you breathing heavily but not out of breath will burn off about 300–500 calories an hour, so it's a great way to lose weight too. Cycle regularly to and from the shops to make small purchases, rather than doing a big shop once a week. Or you could even try cycling to and from work. The Bike2Work scheme allows employees to buy cycles and cycling equipment at a reduced cost; why not persuade your employer to join?

Many towns have cycling clubs which do regular weekend outings of varying lengths – see if yours has one, and if it doesn't why not set one up?

It helps increase your motivation if you record your exercise progress, log how long you exercised for and, crucially, how good you felt afterwards. Keep a record in your well-being journal.

- Physical exercise is a very effective way to lift mood in the short term and improve well-being over the long term.

- Exercise is cheap, if not completely free.

- The physical and mental health benefits of exercise are very wide-ranging and include increased self-esteem, better sleep, improved brain function and reduced stress and depression.

- You can improve your intention to exercise by focusing on how good you'll feel during your workout and afterwards, rather than focusing on how you'll feel at the start.

- Exercising with a friend or as part of a team can increase your commitment, and decrease the chance that you'll drop out if the going gets tough.

- You can also improve and expand your willpower by exercising it.

---

19. Resilience

Our greatest glory is not in never falling, but in rising every time we fall.

Confucius

As I mentioned earlier, sometimes positive psychology has been criticized for its positive focus; people mistakenly believe that this means we never consider the negatives, which of course is not the case. We all know that life has its downs as well as ups, and it would be completely unrealistic to suggest otherwise.

Unfortunately all of us at some time will have to deal with adverse events or experiences. But how and why do some people survive and grow stronger as a result of misfortune, and even thrive on the challenge, whereas others crumble at the slightest setback? Is there a way of increasing our capacity to manage, cope with and overcome unexpected obstacles, be they minor disappointments or major crises?

Developing resilience is a key element of positive psychology since it contributes to your well-being and your ability to live a good life. In this chapter we'll look at some of the evidence behind psychological resilience and try some of the techniques which have been shown to make a difference. So if you want to understand how to make setbacks less problematic, reduce their impact or make them easier to overcome, read on.

When we talk about resilience, we're referring to our ability to keep going in the face of difficulty, to bounce back from adversity and to manage our negative emotions more effectively, rather than letting them drag us into a downward spiral. Often we think of resilience as being a personality trait or characteristic that some people are born with and others not. However you'll be interested to hear that there is growing scientific evidence that resilience is a skill which can be learned. I train the award-winning Bounce Back Resilience and Well-being programme (Reception to Year 8) to teachers and others who work with children and young people (for more information on Bounce Back, see the Resources section). In the USA, the army is being trained in resilience techniques in the Comprehensive Soldier Fitness programme, which has 'strong minds, strong bodies' as its strapline. We expect soldiers to be trained to the peak of physical health, the argument goes, so why not the peak of mental health too?

Benefits of resilience

Interestingly, resilience has knock-on benefits for both your psychological and physical health. Resilient people are those who:

- Are more likely to perceive challenges and setbacks as manageable
- Have greater emotional stability
- Have greater ability to cope with both major stressors and daily hassles

- Have greater zest and energy for life
- Are curious and open to new experiences
- Are good at helping other people feel good too (which is great for building relationships).

Additionally, resilience helps to counterbalance the physical effects of stress on the human body. Imagine being told that you have to give a public speech with little time for preparation and that your performance will be scored. In this kind of situation, even if we manage to maintain a calm exterior, most of us would feel pretty stressed on the inside, and our heart rate and blood pressure would rocket. In laboratory experiments, the heart rate and blood pressure of resilient people return to normal more quickly in these kinds of situations – in other words, resilience helps to offset the effects of experiencing negative emotions and stress.

Researchers also suggest that being resilient in one domain of life (e.g. work) can help in another (e.g. relationships).

So, what kind of things can you do to boost your level of resilience, and put you back on the road to recovery after a disappointment or setback? One thing we often forget is that we already have a wealth of experience on which we can draw. All of us will have experienced setback, rejection and challenge of various degrees at some stage in our lives, so it's worthwhile reflecting on what we did to get back on an even keel at the time. Reflecting in this way helps reinforce that we already have resources at our disposal, whether that's our own internal characteristics and traits, such as creativity or persistence, or external resources such as support from family and friends.

Survival strategies

Spend 5–10 minutes reflecting on your life so far. What challenges or disappointments have you already successfully overcome? Perhaps you have experienced personal rejection, redundancy or failed an important exam. Any of these events may be fertile ground for learning about your own resilience and ways of bouncing back. Choose one event to focus on. In your well-being journal, write down:

- Briefly what happened – just the facts
- How you coped – specifically what you did that helped you manage the negative emotions at the time, and enabled you to bounce back successfully. What strengths did you draw on? Which coping mechanisms did you use? Who did you ask for help?
- How you felt at the time and how differently you feel about it now
- What you have learned about your existing level of resilience that is useful to you now.

Note: it's important in this exercise to focus *only* on an event or experience which you know you have successfully overcome. Don't choose anything you are ambivalent about, or which feels raw or otherwise unresolved.

Dear diary

Psychology research also suggests that people who write about their worst life experiences report greater physical and psychological well-being, in terms of improved life satisfaction and health, compared to those who merely think privately about their experiences.[26] This may be because writing requires you to structure and organize your thoughts more carefully and allows you to process the negative emotions that accompanied the life event, whereas just thinking about it can be more random and may result in negative rumination.

Resilience in 3D: distract, distance and dispute

Three other useful techniques for building resilience are the 'three Ds': distraction, distancing and disputation.[27] We have already covered disputation in some depth in Chapter 17 – you may wish to refresh your memory now.

Distraction involves doing something quickly to calm or silence your negative inner voice before it gets a real grip. As mentioned in Chapter 17, the way we explain what happens to us determines whether we are an optimist or a pessimist. When bad things happen, pessimists explain them in a 'me, always, everything' way. Distraction techniques, such as focusing your attention on an external physical object, such as the pen in your hand or a picture on the wall, and telling yourself loudly to 'stop', are ways of interrupting these negative thought patterns before they envelop and overwhelm you. Once you start ruminating on a negative situation you need a will of iron to stop yourself, so early distraction is the key.

However, it may be that these simple distractions are not enough for you to regain your composure completely, and your negative inner voice may start up again. If so, buy yourself some time, and do something to change your mood. You can distract yourself in many other ways, for example, socializing, immersing yourself in a favourite hobby, walking the dog or making a cup of tea. Afterwards you may feel more able to reflect on the disappointment objectively.

Distancing will also help improve your resilience. Distancing means reminding yourself that the way you interpret what goes on around you is just that, an interpretation, not necessarily the true facts.

As scientist and philosopher Alfred Korzybski once said, 'a map is not the territory'. In other words, what we perceive as reality is not the same thing as reality – other people may have other interpretations which may be as valid, or more valid, than our own. Remembering this can take some of the emotional sting out of a rejection, disappointment or setback.

You might also try asking yourself questions such as:

- Will this (the negative event or experience) matter in 5 hours/days/weeks/years time?

- Who is worse off than me at this precise moment in time?
- What else could happen that would be worse than this?
- What else do I have in my life (e.g. family, friends, career, health etc.) that is unaffected by this?
- How else might I interpret this situation more positively?

Another good distancing technique is to think of someone whose level-headedness and composure in trying times you respect, and imagine how they would respond in the same situation. If they were in your shoes, what would they say, feel and do differently?

Disputation involves looking for the evidence for and against your negative belief or explanation, then finding alternative, equally valid (or possibly more valid) inter-pretations. The detailed process for disputing is set out in Chapter 17.

Some people find it helpful to write down evidence for and against in two columns on a page, with their negative explanation on one side and the various positive reframes on the other. Try this now in your well-being journal.

If you cannot decide whether there is more evidence for a positive explanation than a negative one, clinical psychol-ogist Alan Carr suggests asking yourself which explanation or belief would be *most useful* to you in terms of regaining your positive mood and achieving your goals.

Closed doors, open doors

When one door closes another door opens; but we so often look so long and so regretfully upon the closed door, that we do not see the ones which open for us.

Alexander Graham Bell

Often when something negative happens, our feelings of regret and disappointment overwhelm us to the extent that we become blind to other opportunities which then appear. The trick here is to contain our negative emotions so that they don't spill over, increase in intensity or drag us into a downward spiral, and then to try looking at the problem as a challenge to be overcome. Psychologists call this benefit-finding. Resilient people are more adept at finding, or noticing, the 'open doors'.

Psychologist Tayyab Rashid recommends spending time looking for doors which have opened as a result of others closing.

 Think of a time in your life when you have experienced a big disappointment (this might be the same event or experience you used in the survival strategies activity, or something different). Reflect on what new opportunities arose after this door closed. In your well-being journal answer the following questions:

- How long did it take you to see the new opportunity?
- What, if anything, prevents you from seeing new opportunities?
- What can you do to improve your ability to notice new opportunities?
- Finally, reflect on how overcoming this negative event or experience has influenced your life for the better.

 Carrie had worked as a middle manager in a medium-sized engineering company for 11 years. She enjoyed her job very much and had no intention of leaving. A series of lost contracts meant that the firm had to find big cost savings, and Carrie, along with about 20 others, was made redundant. Initially this was a bitter blow and after leaving the firm she fell into depression. Then one day, reading a magazine in the dentist's waiting room, she came across an article about women who had successfully changed careers. On her way home she noticed a spring in her step: it was the first time in many months that she had felt so hopeful. Over the next few weeks, inspired by the stories she'd read, she explored the option of teacher training, which she'd considered after leaving university but hadn't pursued. Two years later, Carrie has just completed her first term of classroom experience, and is loving every minute of it. 'Being made redundant was one of the worst things that ever happened to me,' she said, 'And it's also one of the best. If I hadn't lost my management job back then, I know I wouldn't be where I am now, doing my teaching practical and on course to qualifying as a science teacher. It just shows that every cloud has a silver lining.'

THINGS TO REMEMBER!

- Resilience is a skill which can be learned.

- There are numerous resilience-building techniques to choose from, so you will be able to find some which suit you.

- Resilience has enormous benefits for both your physical and psychological well-being.

- The key to resilience and bouncing back after adversity is to change your explanatory style – that is, modify pessimistic thoughts and beliefs so that your explanatory style is more optimistic.

- As with any other skill, practice makes perfect!

20. Savouring

The aim of life is appreciation.

G.K. Chesterton

Appreciation crops up a lot in positive psychology. Remember that we looked at three different meanings of appreciation in Chapter 8, and explored gratitude in some depth in Chapter 12.

Savouring is a more down-to-earth definition of appreciation which covers all three senses of the word: to be thankful for something, to acknowledge the quality of something and to increase in value. In positive psychology terminology, savouring is about really *noticing, appreciating and enhancing* the positive experiences in your life. By savouring you slow down and consciously pay attention to all your senses (touch, taste, sight, sound and smell). You stretch out the experience, and concentrate on noticing what it is that you really enjoy, whether it's sipping a glass of chilled champagne, looking forward to collecting your child from nursery, or recollecting the time you scored a hat-trick for the office football team. Through learning to savour, you can increase your capacity to notice what is good about your life, as well as appreciate it more fully.

Evolutionary psychology suggests that humans have an inbuilt survival mechanism called the negativity bias which means that we tend to notice bad things in life before we see the good things (see more about this in Chapter 2). By learning techniques to counteract this negativity bias you can increase your well-being. Savouring is one such strategy. And because savouring comes in a variety of forms, all of which are geared towards intensifying the positive experiences you have, there will be at least one technique which works for you.

Ways to savour

Savouring comes in many different varieties. Start with this simple exercise: what synonyms for the word 'savouring' can you think of? Jot them down in your well-being journal.

Did you come up with any of the following?

- Relishing
- Cherishing
- Treasuring
- Revelling
- Basking
- Luxuriating
- Marvelling
- Revering
- Delighting

Spend 5 minutes thinking about what kind of thing you would be doing if you were luxuriating, or basking, in something. What would you cherish? What would you revel in? Then turn your attention to the present moment wherever you happen to be as you read this: is there something about your current experience which you can savour?

Psychologists Fred Bryant and Joseph Veroff, the leading experts in the field, argue that savouring encompasses all of the above synonyms.

You will notice from this first exercise that we can find many different ways to extract even more pleasure from positive day-to-day experiences. You may bask in warm sunshine for example, luxuriate in a scented bath, revel in special birthday or Christmas festivities, marvel at a glorious sunset, or treasure a precious memory.

Savouring is not difficult – here's how to do it ...

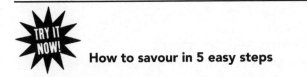

How to savour in 5 easy steps

1. Slow down
2. Pay attention to what you are doing
3. Use all your senses
4. S-t-r-e-t-c-h out the experience
5. Reflect on your enjoyment.

It's important to remember that savouring is a process not an outcome – in other words it's something we do, not something we get.

Bryant and Veroff suggest that there are many different ways in which you can savour experiences:

- You can savour things *in the present moment*, such as eating a favourite food
- You can savour things *from the past*, such as reminiscing about a happy childhood or holiday

- You can savour things *in the future*, for example, anticipating your graduation ceremony, or the birth of a grandchild.

Why not try all three modes? It may be that you're more comfortable with one particular one, and that's absolutely fine.

Tell me more, tell me more!

This is an exercise to do in pairs. If your partner is at home, ask them to join you. Or if you're at work, you can do this in a lunch break with a colleague, or over the phone with a good friend.

Each of you should take a piece of paper and a pencil. Next, quickly jot down a list of the happiest experiences of your life, maybe 3–5 of them. Each choose one happy experience that you can easily share with the other person. Take it in turns to describe it in detail. Where were you? What was going on? What were you doing? Who else was there? What made it such a memorable and positive experience? How did it make you feel then? How does it make you feel now, looking back? Tell me more! Really try to picture being there again, and bask or luxuriate in the positive memories that are created by this reminiscing.

When it's your partner's turn, your role as the listener is to help them savour every aspect of the story as they recount it, by listening actively and asking questions that will amplify the positive memories for them.

Anticipate eagerly

This exercise is very simple – it's similar to 'Tell me more!' although you can do this one alone if you wish.

Think of a positive experience or event which is *in the future* – perhaps you're going on a date at the weekend, or you have a party to look forward to, or a good friend is visiting.

Imagine how the event or experience will pan out in as much detail as you can. Where will you be? What clothes will you wear? Who else will be there? What will you do? Picture it in your mind's eye as clearly as you can. What positive feelings do you notice as you visualize this experience? Excitement? Curiosity? Joy? Love? Take time to relish these positive emotions.

The 3 Es

Remember how excited, enthusiastic and expressive you were as a child when good things happened? Perhaps 'Wow!' was one of your favourite expressions. Or 'Awesome!', 'Fab!' or 'Wicked!'

As we go through our teenage years some of us lose the capacity to express ourselves positively with the same passion. It becomes un-cool, and we slowly forget how. So next time you feel really good about something, why not throw caution to the wind and dance for joy, punch the air or whoop with delight? It may not feel like you to start with, but with a little practice you can re-capture some of the natural ebullience that you had as a child. This is sometimes called 'faking it till you make it'. There is evidence that expressing your positive feelings externally can intensify them, so why not give it a go?

Savour the flavour!

As I mentioned in Chapters 13 and 16, food can play a big part in your journey towards greater happiness and contentment. Savouring is a form of appreciation, and eating and drinking are great ways to practise your savouring technique. Often we're so busy that we eat and drink on the move, grabbing handy snacks as we go. We wish that we weren't always in such a rush, but give little thought to how we might slow down, other than dreaming of an early retirement!

This activity works well with soft summer fruits such as strawberries or blueberries, or with chocolate, though you can choose to savour any food you like. The idea is to eat it as *slowly* as possibly, whilst using all of your senses to prolong the positive experience and draw the maximum pleasure from it. Make sure you're sitting where you won't be interrupted for 5 minutes.

- First of all, slow down! Pick up your strawberry and admire it: take your time to notice its unique colour, shape and smell. Notice all the little seeds on its surface and the bright green of the stalk. Focus all your senses intently on it.

- How does the strawberry smell? Is it strong or subtle, sweet or spicy? Close your eyes and breathe in the aroma.

What pleasant memories does it conjure up? Perhaps the lazy days of summer, or long childhood holidays. Linger over these memories. Enjoy the anticipation!

- Take a small bite of the strawberry, noticing the texture in your mouth, as well as the taste. Chew as slowly as you can, noticing the myriad of tastes being released, and allowing its full flavour to develop on your tongue. Relish it!

- Finally swallow, noticing any further pleasurable sensations as you do so.

- Repeat, this time even more slowly.

So, how did that feel? How was that different to how you normally eat? It's likely that this experience of savouring food is nothing like your usual way of eating.

Savouring is similar to mindfulness (Chapter 13), but it's a narrower concept. When eating mindfully you remain totally open to and aware of both external and internal stimuli, whereas when savouring your food, you focus specifically on pleasurable sensations.

It's easier to savour food if you remove other distractions – so don't eat when you're driving, watching TV, listening to the radio, chatting or reading. Focus solely on the food itself, and close your eyes. You'll notice that when you savour it, food seems to last longer and you enjoy it far more.

How not to savour!

There are several things which can completely spoil your experience of savouring, or fail to get it off the ground. These include:

- Killjoy thinking, such as thinking about how the experience might be improved
- Analysing in the moment why an experience is positive
- Rushing.

- It's difficult to savour things if you're in a hurry, so take your time.

- *Attend* to the experience, using *all* your senses – touch, taste, sight, smell, sound.

- Don't try to work out whether or why you're enjoying something.

- You can savour things in the past, in the present and in the future.

- You can savour alone, or you can share the experience with someone else.

- Savouring is a process (i.e. something you do) not an outcome.

- There are many different ways to savour; there will be at least one savouring technique which suits you. But why not try them all?

---

21. Positive psychology of time

Life is what happens to you while you're busy making other plans.

John Lennon

Our lives, certainly in the Western world, are dominated by time. Think about it for a moment; how many activities do you do where time isn't an important factor? I bet there aren't that many. At work and at home, time and how we use it takes centre stage, whether it's 2 minutes to clean your teeth, a 45-minute commute to work, a 2 hour meeting, a 10-minute ready meal or 3 minutes of extra time when your side is losing. In this chapter we'll be exploring two different aspects of time – time use and time perspectives – and looking at their importance and relevance to our well-being.

Time use

The perception that we are short of time is all around us. Media messages continually remind us how busy we are, how hard we work, how little free time we have and how we need to get some 'work-life balance'. It's so obvious that we don't have enough time that we don't even question it. Yet studies suggest that people underestimate the amount of free time they have in a week by about half. According to researchers John Robinson and Geoffrey Godbey,

Americans of working age actually have as much free time in a week as they have work time; about 35 hours.

 Did you know that the total number of hours that the average British employee works in their lifetime has shrunk from 124,000 (in 1856) to 69,000 (in 1981)? This is even more astonishing when you consider that the average length of a career has not changed – it's still about 40 years.

Research suggests that in 1870 the average British worker worked 2,984 hours per year. By 1938 this had decreased to 2,267 hours, and by 1987 it was only 1,557 hours.

During the same period of time, total non-work hours have increased from 118,000 in 1856 to 287,000 in 1981. Part of this increase in non-work hours is attributable to longer life expectancy, and therefore a greater number of non-work hours in retirement. Nevertheless it means that whilst we might think we're working harder than ever, the figures don't bear this out.

So, now that we have substantially more leisure time than at any point in our working history, what are we doing with this time, and are we putting it to good use?

It's strange when you look at the bare facts, since many people think they are working longer hours than ever, and have far less leisure time. So why do people underestimate the amount of free time they have each week by half? What is contributing to the feeling that we're more time pressured than ever before? Positive psychologist Dr Ilona Boniwell suggests that one of the reasons may be because we try to do too many things. A good example of this is my friend Laura, who has two school-age daughters. Not content with one after-school club for them, she regularly ferries them to two and sometimes even three in the same day! Megan does hockey practice followed by extra maths and a violin lesson on Wednesdays; Sophie goes to art club, then choir practice and swimming. Boniwell suggests that squeezing in so many activities leaves us feeling very pressed for time, and contributes to the feeling that we are rushing to get things done, even though we actually have more free hours at our disposal than ever before.

 Estimate how much leisure time you have each week (by 'leisure time' we mean time when you're not doing paid or unpaid work, sleeping, eating or looking after the kids): _____ hours per week

Now keep a simple diary in your well-being journal every day for a week or so, noting briefly what you spend your time doing, and accounting for every single hour.

What do you notice about your leisure time? Do you have more or less than you initially thought? If this is a typical week, what do you spend most of your leisure time doing? Does your use of leisure time increase or decrease your well-being? If the latter, how could you use it differently?

The time thief

Trends in TV-viewing are quite alarming. According to time-use studies, television viewing time in European countries at the end of the 1990s averaged between 2 and 2.75 hours per day, with a fifth of people saying that they watch TV for more than 3 hours per day. Research from TV ratings agencies themselves suggests that people fritter away an even larger proportion of their free time in front of the goggle-box (in Europe about 3.5 hours per day on average, and in the US, 4.5 hours), and these figures seem to be constantly increasing. Now, what's wrong with that, you may ask? It's a free country after all, and no-one is making us sit there and absorb hour upon hour of reality TV, soap or docu-drama. Plus, watching the telly can be both very entertaining and relaxing, and 3 hours or so is not a lot to spend on the sofa after a hard day's slog at the office, is it?

Psychologists argue that we're not actually making a rational choice when we slump in front of the TV for the evening. For a start we get the benefits of TV-watching, such as being entertained, immediately, whereas the 'costs', such as not getting enough sleep or not investing enough time in our relationships, are in the future. And we also have a self-control problem. When push comes to shove, although we all generally acknowledge that yes, OK, we do watch more TV than is good for us, we don't often do very much about it!

But is there anything wrong with watching TV anyway? Surprisingly, we don't rate it very highly in the happiness-inducing stakes – it comes out at below average or about average for enjoyment. Secondly, whilst it can seem to make time pass very quickly, watching TV isn't challenging enough to induce a flow state (see Chapter 4) and improve our well-being that way. Thirdly, people who watch lots of television place more importance on affluence (possibly because they see a lot of celebrities on the small screen), are less satisfied with their financial situation, feel less safe, trust other people less and think that they see their friends less than their peers. 3.5 hours per day adds up to *over 3 working days every week* – now that's one hell of a lot of spare time to squander on an activity which doesn't give us that much pleasure. There must be other ways to spend our time which are more likely to make us happy.

What was your leisure time tally?

Tell yourself that next time you catch yourself aimlessly hopping from channel to channel, you're going to switch off and spend the time on your favourite hobby, whatever that might be.

To make this easier, you need to be a little prepared; having made the decision to tear yourself away from the TV and plunge yourself into cake-baking for an hour, nothing will be more demotivating and likely to get you back on that sofa with the remote-control clutched tightly in your hand than finding you have none of the essential ingredients in your cupboard. So try to plan ahead. Your well-being is worth the effort.

Time perspective

OK. Say you've done your time-use diary for a week or so and have made a few changes to how you spend your free time. What if you still feel as if your work-life balance is out of control? How can you avoid feeling that the hours and days are racing past and start feeling as if you're in control of your time again? The answer may lie in your time perspective (TP). By TP, we mean whether you're typically living in and focused on the present, the past or the future.

Psychologists Philip Zimbardo and Ilona Boniwell have researched the subject of time perspectives and their relationship to our well-being. Your time perspective is important because it has a powerful influence on your decision making and the subsequent actions that you take.

There are 5 main TPs:

Future time perspective: if you have a future TP you're able to delay gratification and work towards future rewards. People with a future TP tend to be more successful than others.

Present positive time perspective: if you have this TP you're very focused on enjoying life to the max in the here and now. You're less likely to be concerned about the consequences of your actions.

Present negative time perspective: this TP is characterized by a sense of hopelessness. You believe that your life is controlled by outside forces rather than by you.

Past positive time perspective: if you have this TP you get a lot of pleasure from looking back over your life and reminiscing. You like to maintain family traditions.

Past negative time perspective: you're more focused on what you should have done differently in your life and you're likely to have many regrets.

Which TP describes you best? And which TP would you say is more likely to lead to higher well-being?

Research suggests that the TP most conducive to well-being is the **past positive**, although Zimbardo and Boniwell opt for what they call the **balanced time perspective**, which means that you take the best from past, present and future TPs, rather than slavishly following one over any other.

Which TP do you favour?
You may like to log on to Philip Zimbardo's website and take the Zimbardo Time Perspective

Inventory (ZTPI), comparing your results to the 'ideal' (or 'balanced') time perspective:

thetimeparadox.com/zimbardo-time-perspective -inventory

Benefits of a having a balanced time perspective (BTP)

Researchers have found that people who have a BTP:

- Are happier
- Are more satisfied with life
- Experience more positive emotions
- Have a stronger sense of life purpose
- Are more effective
- Are more optimistic.

TP reflection
Spend 10–15 minutes reflecting on the results from your ZTPI and answer the following questions:

- Do you recognize yourself in your ZTPI score?
- Do you have one dominant time perspective, or a mixture of several?
- How does your dominant TP (or TPs) show up in your life?
- Does your dominant TP (or TPs) work for you?

The key to achieving a more balanced time perspective is being able to adopt the TP which is most appropriate to the situation you're in. Awareness of the various TPs is a great starting point. If you have one or two TPs which dominate, you can practise switching between them.

For example, it's generally helpful whilst you're working or studying to maintain a future TP, but it can make you feel restless and anxious if you're still focused on the future when you get home or have a day off. To maximize your enjoyment of family and leisure time, adopting a present positive TP is more helpful.

If you tend to have a dominant future TP, next time you are with your family and friends, switch off from work and focus your full attention on them. The practice of mindfulness (Chapter 13) can help you develop a more present positive TP.

If you tend to have a dominant present positive TP, try sitting down for 20–30 minutes and making some longer term plans. See Chapter 15 on goal-setting too.

If you are low on the past positive TP, give an old friend a ring or browse through some holiday snaps.

In order to create a more balanced time perspective, you need to practise being able to switch from one TP to another, so that you can adopt the one which is most appropriate for the situation you find yourself in.

THINGS TO REMEMBER!

- Even though we often feel pressed for time, on average we work fewer hours and have more leisure time than ever before in our history.

- The average European squanders as much as 21 hours per week of their precious leisure time in front of the television.

- Your time perspective (TP) – the way you think about and relate to time in your life – is essential to your well-being.

- A balanced time perspective is most conducive to well-being.

- You can learn to develop a more balanced time perspective.

22. Where next?

Well, here we are at the end of *A Practical Guide to Positive Psychology*. I hope that this book has given you the insight into the world of positive psychology that you were looking for, that it has motivated you to do some of the suggested exercises and activities to increase your well-being and that it has inspired you to discover even more about the subject. If that's the case, there is a list of the main websites on positive psychology in the Resources section. Remember that as the field gains in importance, new research and books on the subject are being published all the time.

The aim of this book was to cover the most important topics and theories within the science of positive psychology, human happiness and well-being, as well as to outline some of the practical applications which you could try in your own time. When it comes to well-being, theory alone is not enough. The reason that the activities have played such a major role in the book is because research evidence suggests that as much as 40 per cent of our happiness comes from the things that we do and the day-to-day choices we make. This is very good news; it means that each of us can do something to improve our own level of well-being. So if you have been a little unsure about trying any of the suggested activities, I'd urge you to reconsider. Remember too that feeling outside of your comfort zone occasionally is a good thing; it's a sign that you're learning something new.

At the same time, it's worth reiterating that some of the exercises and activities may not be right for you, and that's fine too; just continue the ones which work for you. Although this book is based on scientific findings, every one of us is unique and what may suit one person under experimental conditions may not suit the next. It's a matter of personal choice as well as individual likes and dislikes. What I suggest is that you try all the activities at least a couple of times before you decide whether or not you'll continue with them over the longer term.

At the start of this book I recommended that you approached it as a mini research project, with you as the subject of the experiment, assessing your well-being at the start by using one of the scientifically validated well-being questionnaires, then carrying out some of the exercises and activities that I've described. I also suggested that you start keeping a well-being journal, in which to record the activities you choose, and your progress, as well as any reflections or observations. Greater self-awareness is an immense asset when it comes to improving your well-being; discovering more about yourself and your responses to life's events and experiences can be tremendously useful.

Now that you've reached the end of the book, you might consider re-assessing your well-being with the same questionnaires you used at the start, to see how your well-being has improved. There are two important points to remember when you're thinking about your own happiness. Firstly, a life full of soaring positive emotion such as bliss, ecstasy and rapture is simply not possible; all of us, at some point or other, will have to endure disappointments and setbacks, as well as sadness at loss or anger at injustice. Accepting that life does have its inevitable ups and downs is a great step forward, and the research behind positive psychology can help us all make the best of the ups and limit the emotional impact of the downs.

The second point to remember is that the instant differences you experience are likely to be relatively short-term lifts in mood and emotion; long-lasting personal change, such as decreasing a pessimistic outlook and increasing an optimistic one, will take consistent motivation, self-control and effort over time. The key message from the science of positive psychology is very clear – achieving lasting improvements in your well-being means you doing little things differently every day.

A Practical Guide to Positive Psychology has provided you with the basic theories and concepts, as well as plenty of ideas for new and interesting activities which you can try. Now it's over to you. What one thing can you do *today* that will help improve your well-being for the longer term?

Resources

In this section you'll find a selection of positive psychology-related websites and other information on the subjects of happiness and well-being.

Websites

workmad.co.uk
On our website you can find further relevant and practical information about positive psychology, including:

- All the references used in this book and suggestions for further reading about Positive Psychology
- Details of our two-day Positive Psychology Masterclasses where you can learn to apply Positive Psychology for your personal and professional development
- Details of the award-winning Bounce Back Resilience and Well-being Training for schools, as well as other positive psychology-based workshops and consultancy
- A regular blog about applying positive psychology

anglia.ac.uk/study/postgraduate-taught/applied -positive-psychology
Details of the new International Masters in Applied Positive Psychology (MSc) programme, taking place at Anglia Ruskin University in Cambridge and Centre d'Études Diplomatiques et Stratégiques in Paris.

actionforhappiness.org

Action for Happiness is a movement to create positive social change, launched by the Young Foundation (**young foundation.org**) in 2011. The website contains lots of useful resources such as the '10 Keys to Happier Living' and video clips from various scientists and researchers in the field of positive psychology and well-being, as well as postings on what works for them by members of the public who have joined Action for Happiness. Action for Happiness is free to join.

positivepsychology.org

This is the website for the University of Pennsylvania's Positive Psychology Center, directed by Martin Seligman. It's full of useful positive psychology research, initiatives and questionnaires such as the VIA Inventory of Strengths (VIA-IS, covered in Chapter 9), the Satisfaction with Life Scale (SWLS) and the Positive and Negative Affect Scale (PANAS). You do have to register in order to be able to use these questionnaires, but don't worry, this is for academic research purposes only.

centreforconfidence.co.uk

The Centre for Confidence and Well-being is a not-for-profit organization set up in 2005 to improve the level of well-being in Scotland. The website provides information and research about key positive psychology subjects such as happiness, optimism, resilience and mindsets. The centre's chief executive, Carol Craig, writes a regular blog on various topics related to positive psychology, including current affairs.

ippanetwork.org
This is the website for the International Positive Psychology Association. IPPA's mission is threefold:

- To promote the science of positive psychology and its research-based applications
- To facilitate collaboration among researchers, teachers, students, and practitioners of positive psychology around the world and across academic disciplines
- To share the findings of positive psychology with the broadest possible audience.

IPPA's members include researchers, students and practitioners of positive psychology as well as members of the general public who have an interest in the field. Membership benefits include reduced conference fees and access to psychology journals.

positivepsychologynews.com
Positive Psychology News Daily is the world's first online journal for news relating to positive psychology. Its authors are primarily graduates of the Universities of Pennsylvania and East London Masters in Applied Positive Psychology programmes, with occasional contributions from guest authors. Topics include coverage of the latest positive psychology research, as well as book and conference reviews, and current affairs. Readers are invited to leave their comments on the articles posted.

neweconomics.org

The New Economics Foundation ('economics as if people and the planet mattered') is a UK-based independent 'think-and-do tank' which aims to improve quality of life by challenging mainstream thinking on economic, environmental and social issues. Its National Accounts of Well-being (**www.nationalaccountsofwellbeing.org**) are inspired. NEF challenges the traditional GDP-based measures of success and social progress by using comprehensive data from a well-being survey of 22 European nations to construct the first ever set of national well-being indicators.

cappeu.com

The Centre for Applied Positive Psychology (CAPP) was founded by Alex Linley in 2005. It focuses on providing strengths-based consultancy to organizations. You'll also find a link on the website to the online R2 strengths assessment tool (covered in Chapter 9).

strengthscope.com

This UK website is the home of the online Strengthscope™ strengths assessment tool mentioned in Chapter 9. You can find plenty of information here about Strengthscope™, including technical data about its validity and reliability.

internationaljournalofwellbeing.org

The International Journal of Well-being is an open access academic journal which was launched to promote inter-disciplinary research on well-being. The IJW is sponsored by the Open Polytechnic of New Zealand. Articles include well-being and trust, public policy, savouring, goals, life satisfaction and 'felicitators' (producers of happiness). As well as articles, the IJW includes expert insights and book reviews.

viacharacter.org
This is the website for the non-profit VIA Institute on character, where you can find the free VIA Strengths assessment.

howsyourday.today
Here you'll find details of the How's Your Day app, which allows you to track your happiness and gives you other evidence-based suggestions to increase it.

appreciativeinquiry.case.edu
For further information, ideas and resources related to Appreciative Inquiry, see the AI Commons portal, hosted by Case Western Reserve University, USA.

uel.ac.uk/Postgraduate/Courses/MSc-Applied-Positive -Psychology-and-Coaching-Psychology
This is the website for the University of East London's MSc in Applied Positive Psychology and Coaching Psychology programme which was the first Masters programme of its kind in the UK. You can study positive psychology and coaching psychology to Certificate, Diploma or Masters level, over a year full-time, or two years part-time.

bda.uk.com
nutrition.org.uk
eatwell.gov.uk
All three of these websites can be used to find up-to-date research, information and advice about the link between nutrition, well-being and health.

ons.gov.uk/ons/guide-method/user-guidance/
well-being/index.html
The ONS now produces national well-being data to supplement more traditional measures of progress such as gross domestic product (GDP).

bangor.ac.uk/mindfulness/research.php.en
This is the website for the Centre for Mindfulness Research and Practice at the University of Bangor in Wales. Here you can find information about the application of mindfulness in programmes such as mindfulness-based stress reduction (MBSR) and mindfulness-based cognitive therapy (MBCT).

Follow me, find me, friend me

Follow me on Twitter: @Bridgetgc, find me on LinkedIn and friend me on Facebook. By joining me on Twitter and LinkedIn you'll find the most up-to-date information about the subjects of happiness, well-being and strengths in the news, along with the latest research and reports from the field of positive psychology and other related topics. I look forward to hearing from you.

Notes

1. Lyubomirsky, S., Sheldon, K. M., & Schkade, D. (2005), 'Pursuing Happiness: The Architecture of Sustainable Change', *Review of General Psychology*, 9(2): 111–131.

2. James, O. (2009), *Affluenza*, Random House.

3. Lyubomirsky, S., Dickerhoof, R., Boehm, J. K., & Sheldon, K. M. (2011), 'Becoming happier takes both a will and a proper way: An experimental longitudinal intervention to boost well-being', *Emotion*, 11(2): 391–402.

4. Huta, V., Park, N., Peterson, C. & Seligman, M. (2003), 'Pursuing pleasure versus eudaimonia: Which leads to greater satisfaction?' Poster presented at the 2nd International Positive Psychology Summit, Washington DC, USA. Cited in Boniwell, I. (2008), *Positive Psychology in a Nutshell* (second edition), PWBC.

5. Schueller, S. M., & Seligman, M. P. (2010), 'Pursuit of pleasure, engagement, and meaning: Relationships to subjective and objective measures of well-being', *Journal of Positive Psychology*, 5(4): 253–263.

6. Seligman, M. (2011), *Flourish*, Nicolas Brealey Publishing.

7. Diener, E., & Seligman, M. P. (2002), 'Very happy people', *Psychological Science*, 13(1): 81–84.

8. Rozin, P., & Royzman, E. B. (2001), 'Negativity bias, negativity dominance, and contagion', *Personality and Social Psychology Review*, 5(4): 296–320.

9. Solnick, S. & Hemenway , D. (1998), 'Is more always better? A survey on positional concerns', *Journal of Economic Behaviour and Organisation*, 37: 373–83.

10. Lucas, R. E., & Clark, A. E. (2006), 'Do people really adapt to marriage?', *Journal of Happiness Studies*, 7(4): 405–426

11. Fredrickson, B.L. (2009), *Positivity*, Crown.

12. Brown, N. J., Sokal, A. D., & Friedman, H. L. (2013), 'The complex dynamics of wishful thinking: The critical positivity ratio', *American Psychologist*, 68(9): 801–813.

13. Diener, E., & Seligman, M. (2002), 'Very happy people', *Psychological Science*, 13(1): 81–4.

14. Gable, S. L., Reis, H. T., Impett, E. A., & Asher, E. R. (2004), 'What do you do when things go right? The intrapersonal and interpersonal benefits of sharing positive events', *Journal of Personality and Social Psychology*, 87(2): 228–45.

15. Kashdan, T. B., & McKnight, P. E. (2009), 'Origins of purpose in life: Refining our understanding of a life well lived', *Psihologijske Teme*, 18(2): 303–16.

16. Dutton, J. E., Debebe, G., & Wrzesniewski, A. (1996), 'The re-valuing of de-valued work: The importance of relationships for hospital cleaning staff', Paper presented at the Annual Meeting of the Academy of Management, Cincinnati.

17. Linley, A. (2008), *Average to A+*, CAPP Press.

18. Schwartz, B. (2000), 'Self-determination: The tyranny of freedom', *American Psychologist*, 55: 79–88.

19. Iyengar, S. S., & Lepper, M. R. (2000), 'When choice is demotivating: Can one desire too much of a good thing?' *Journal of Personality and Social Psychology*, 79(6): 995–1006.

20. Lambert, N. M., Graham, S. M., Fincham, F. D., & Stillman, T. F. (2009), 'A changed perspective: How gratitude can affect sense of coherence through positive reframing', *Journal of Positive Psychology*, 4(6):461–470

21. Elliot A. J, Sheldon K. M. (1997), 'Avoidance achievement motivation: a personal goals analysis', *Journal of Personality and Social Psychology*, 73:171–85.

22. Linley, P.A., Maltby, J., Wood, A.M., Joseph, S., Harrington et al. (2007), 'Character strengths in the UK: The VIA Inventory of Strengths', *Personality and Individual Differences*, 43: 341–351.

23. Broadway, J. M., Redick, T. S., & Engle, R. W. (2010), 'Working memory capacity: Self-control is (in) the goal'. In R. R. Hassin, K. N. Ochsner, Y. Trope' (eds.), *Self-control in society, mind, and brain*, Oxford University Press.

24. Akbaraly, T. N., Brunner, E. J., Ferrie, J. E., Marmot, M. G., Kivimaki, M., & Singh-Manoux, A. (2009), 'Dietary pattern and depressive symptoms in middle age', *British Journal of Psychiatry*, 195(5): 408–413.

25. Babyak, M., Blumenthal, J. A., Herman, S., Khatri, P., Doraiswamy, M., & Moore, K. et al. (2000), 'Exercise treatment for major depression: Maintenance of therapeutic benefit at 10 months', *Psychosomatic Medicine*, 62(5): 633–638.

26. Lyubomirsky, S., Sousa, L., & Dickerhoof, R. (2006), 'The costs and benefits of writing, talking, and thinking about life's triumphs and defeats', *Journal of Personality and Social Psychology*, 90(4): 692–708.

27. Seligman, M. (1998), *Learned optimism*, Pocket Books.

Index